ACTING
THROUGH
MASK

Mask: A Release of Acting Resources

A series of books written and illustrated by David Griffiths

Volume 1
Acting through Mask
Written and illustrated by David Griffiths

Volume 2
The Training of Noh Actors and *The Dove*
Written and illustrated by David Griffiths

Volume 3
The Italian Commedia and *Please Be Gentle*
Written and illustrated by David Griffiths

Volume 4
The Masquerades of Nigeria and *Touch*
Written and illustrated by David Griffiths

This book is part of a series. The publisher will accept continuation orders which may be cancelled at any time and which provide for automatic billing and shipping of each title in the series upon publication. Please write for details.

ACTING
THROUGH
MASK

Written and illustrated
by
David Griffiths

harwood academic publishers
Australia • Canada • China • France • Germany • India
Japan • Luxembourg • Malaysia • The Netherlands • Russia
Singapore • Switzerland • Thailand • United Kingdom

Amsteldijk 166
1st Floor
1079 LH Amsterdam
The Netherlands

British Library Cataloguing in Publication Data

Griffiths, David
   Acting through mask. – (Mask: a release of acting
   resources; v. 1)
   1. Masques   2. Acting
   I. Title
   792'.028

   ISBN 3-7186-5714-7

Cover illustrations by David Griffiths.

I dedicate this book to my late parents Jack and Doris,
who initiated and inspired the opportunity,
and to Vicky who supported me unselfishly throughout the period of
research and writing, and shared the joy of its completion.

CONTENTS

CONTENTS

INTRODUCTION TO THE SERIES

Mask: A Release of Acting Resources is a fully illustrated four-volume series, which examines the effect of mask in performance.

This series reflects my practical work and draws upon my research into the secret world of the Noh of Japan and the Masquerade of Nigeria, the comic style of the Commedia Dell'Arte and the training of actors through mask in Britain.

The series also includes my three masked plays called *The Dove, Please Be Gentle* and *Touch*, which transform and test the results of my experiments into theatrical practicality.

David Griffiths

ACKNOWLEDGEMENTS

I would like to thank the following: Dr David Richards for sowing the seed and making the original research enquiry on my behalf; the School of English, University of Leeds, for giving me the opportunity; the British Academy for setting the precedent of offering me an annual award and having faith that it would be used responsibly; Tom Needham for his friendship and his "investment" of £1000, without which I would not have been able to visit Japan; the Society of Friends for their grant of £500, which was given to me at a time of great financial need; all those at the Tramshed in Glasgow who led me to *The Mahabharata* and Peter Brook; Chris and Vayu Banfield who have have embraced me with a continuous stream of encouragement, practical help and invaluable advice; Alan Vaughan Williams, a wonderfully exciting theatre director, who gave me some of my early directing work and who continues to support and encourage without qualification; and Professor Martin Banham who supervised and guided me through my original enquiry with extreme care, the right amount of humour and encouraging portions of excitement.

In Japan, I am eternally grateful for the extraordinary hospitality and kindness given to me by my supervisor Professor Yasunari Takahashi, Jo Barnett CBE (Director of the British Council, Tokyo) and his staff at Kyoto, Chizuko and Naoichi Tsuyama my hosts and dear friends, Richard Emmert, and Fumiye Miho and Friends at the Friends' House in Tokyo.

LIST OF ILLUSTRATIONS

INTRODUCTION

'I have never believed in single truth. Neither my own nor those of others. I believe all schools, all theories can be useful in some place at some time, but I have discovered that one can only live by a passionate, and absolute, identification with a point of view'.

Peter Brook. [1]

It is now six years since I completed a period of research on actor-training at the University of Leeds under the supervision of Professor Martin Banham. I was given a rare opportunity to collate and record in detail almost twenty years of my professional work preparing specialist drama teachers for primary and secondary schools, directing in the theatre especially with young actors and more recently as a playwright.

Since that time I have returned to working in all these areas refreshed and armed with added resources discovered during my period of research. However, the main argument which dominated my thesis six years ago remains intact and uncluttered – if anything, even more stridently declaimed.

'As a result of creating a casebook of practical experiment, and making a detailed examination of the Noh Theatre of Japan, the Commedia Dell'Arte, and the Masquerades of Nigeria, it is my intention to show how the mask, as catalyst and agent, can release and demand those physical elements which form an essential part of the language of Theatre.

These experiments and the resulting information will form the basic resource material for the outline of an alternative programme of actor-training, complementary in its method of vocational preparation, with that of the existing training of performers in Music and Dance'.

In Britain, formal training in Music and Dance often begins before the primary school age and has a syllabus of graded repertoire and practice exercises which anticipate the final, vocational training – requiring a high assessment standard, as a prerequisite of entry – usually at seventeen or

---

[1] Brook, P. *The Shifting Point* (Methuen, 1988) Preface.

eighteen. At this age, in Drama Schools in Britain, an actor will very often be embarking upon the first exploratory introduction to his training.

It is my contention that the somewhat brief, ad hoc facility available for the training of actors in Britain needs an additional programme of skills-based discipline to consolidate and develop its present philosophy if it is to produce actors whose performance skills are as immediately recognisable as those of musicians and dancers.

Despite the many changes in technology and musical innovation, the basic musical training methodology remains relatively unchallenged; similarly with dance. There may be new artistic styles and theory which demand a shift in emphasis in training, but the basic and continuous preparation of body and mind, creation and recreation of repertoire is recognisably apparent and necessary.

The audience attending a recital or ballet have some idea of what has been sacrificed in terms of training and preparation for the performance. There is an expectation of a high level of skill on display. If nothing else there will be ample evidence supporting this expectation.

It is not unusual for teachers of musicians and dancers to remain mentors of their pupils for the duration of their careers. Highly individ-ualistic styles coexist with current and historical trends. This is never a problem, for they all seem to recognise and agree upon a common, basic, training programme, without which the individuality and inspiration of the performer cannot emerge. The repertoire created by choreographers and composers takes account of this common factor in their continuing experimentation with the developing language of their art.

So what is the basis of my disquiet concerning the training and the ensuing performance standards of British actors working within a mainly oral tradition?

My experience of working professionally with actors as teacher and director, has led me to the conclusion that the vast majority of British actors are not sufficiently prepared for the highly complex, artistic demands of theatre performance. What they release in terms of acting skills in order to enrich the artistic sensibility of their audience, can, in my view, be significantly improved.

One of the ways, which would have an immediate effect upon the whole focus of performance skills, is the introduction of a mask-based training philosophy. The mask demands a new and exacting process of learning for the actor by its very presence and the technical skills needed to physically animate it. It is my belief that this philosophy, linked directly to the existing programmes of actor-training, would offer one solution. The mask reference, therefore, is at the centre of this series of books.

Such a programme of mask-based training *is* possible, and can begin at a very young age, continuing and supporting the development of actors throughout their careers. There is ample evidence from other sources to support this view and one prime example is the training methods that prevail for the Noh actor in Japan.

The specific area which I feel needs immediate attention is the methodology surrounding the training of the actor's body.

In this century alone, there has been a continuous lineage of theatre practitioners and teachers in Europe who have devoted much of their working life conducting experiments in actor-training. In Britain, the results of their work are widely known amongst theatre practitioners and teachers but are referred to–occasionally–by only a few.

If one examines the inter-related experiments–both practical and theoretical–of such people as Meyerhold, Stanislavsky, Grotowski, and Peter Brook, the common conclusion which emerges from their work is that the mastery of the craft of acting is only accessible having totally absorbed the skills demanded by that craft. Training takes many years, is extremely demanding and becomes a way of life.

It was to the body in particular, as well as the voice and intellect, that they addressed their attentions, and their common discovery was the release of artistic spontaneity which emerged as a result of their differing programmes of intense and repeated physical training.

They separately determined that whatever the preparation of voice and speech, physical co-ordination and agility, they should be so ingrained on the mind and body of the actor that they become second nature, feeding the conscious demands of the actor as and when they are required.

The implication here is that the actor is standing outside the second-by-second character in performance; a process of spontaneous selection from a pool of resource skills. Like the master of furniture-making, the finished result is usually in direct proportion to the basic skills mastered, and the inspired manner in which these skills have been uniquely applied.

It is not my experience regularly to witness such skills artistically applied by performers in British theatres. What I advocate therefore is an intensive programme in the use of mask in performance by all actors in training, not as an absolute solution, but as a means of access to a theatrical resource which includes a new, physical vocabulary.

Whilst I acknowledge that there has been no mask-based tradition in British theatre since the Mummings and Disguisings of Medieval England and the Court Festivities devised by such playwrights as Ben Jonson, there is strong evidence of a new interest in physical theatre.

This is occasionally exemplified by such innovative companies as the Trestle Theatre Company and Tara Arts who give time and attention to physical, visual and multi-media techniques in their company-devised presentations of masked theatre. But they are a rarity, for in British theatre, the oral tradition tends to dominate the acting style of performance and production.

What I am not advocating is the forming of a new masked tradition in British theatre although this would probably be an inevitable consequence of such a programme of mask training. I am convinced that years of training to work in mask lays the foundations for performing *without* mask. It refocuses the premise upon which an actor subjugates himself to the form, rhythm, and sound of the character he is playing by having the consummate skill to stand outside it and responding technically to recreate its novelty.

One of the most notable devotees of the influence of the mask on performer and audience was Edward Gordon Craig. On 3rd February, 1909, he wrote in his Daybook:

> '... I wish to remove the actor with his personality but to leave the Chorus of Masked Figures... To cover an actor's face with a mask depersonalises him... it compels him to pay attention to his movements, to rely upon his physical means of expression... to recreate rather than reproduce...' [2]

I support this view. This is where I open my investigation.

---

[2] Craig, E. G. *The Mask, The Actor, and The Über-Marionette* (Vol. I, 1908–1909, Florence).

1

A BRIEF EXAMINATION OF
ACTOR-TRAINING EXPERIMENTS
AND STYLE DEVELOPMENTS

STANISLAVSKY, Konstantin Sergeivich (1863–1938)

'How does a singer, a pianist, a dancer, start his day?'
                                                    (Stanislavsky)[1]

Most of Stanislavsky's writing on acting was completed in the last decade of his life, and yet there is no sense of a petrified, retrospective view. His voice in *An Actor Prepares* is one of a deeply passionate and brilliant teacher, who searches for the innate potential of the individual. He advocates a methodology which he has developed and devised as a result of his professional theatrical experience as actor, director, and teacher over the previous forty years. In the sequel, *Building A Character* completed shortly before his death, he writes with the same voice, the same care, and yet – like all committed teachers – he demonstrates his need to explore and realign his theatrical perspective.

His direction to his acting pupils – his philosophy – is crystal clear: an actor must carry with him to his daily ritual of rehearsal and performance a highly trained, physical, vocal and emotionally rich instrument.

His physical development must be as demanding as the training of a gymnast or acrobat and as 'rigorous as a ballet-dancer... which helps to refine physical motions, broadens them, gives them a definition and finish' developing 'a healthy body, in good working order, capable of beauty, proportion, balance... a proper overall form... extraordinary control... physical intuition and inspiration'.[2]

Not that he encourages anything which can be deemed melodramatically extravagant, producing 'affectation, posturing and other such dangerous results'.[3]

---

[1] Stanislavsky, C. *Building a Character* (Translated by E. R. Hapgood. Reinhardt, London, 1950 Third Impression) p. 259.
[2] Stanislavsky, C. pp. 36–38.   [3] Stanislavsky, C. p. 45.

5

He advocates a physical agility which complements exactly the spoken rhythms and dynamics of speech: 'when an actor adds the vivid ornament of sound to that living content of the words'.[4]

If an actor's vocal capacity is compared to the technical intricacies and delights of music, then he must have 'the power to direct his sounds, command their obedience, know that they will forcibly convey the minutest details, modulations, shadings of his creativeness'.[5]

His constant reference to the musicality of words and their meaning, and the technical skills needed to realise the nuances of the text, are revealed in his stress upon the importance of the grammatical structure of language, the power of the pause, the 'hypnotic' comma, the 'eloquent' silence, intonation, accentuation, words 'underscored', and the many layers of subtext.

Such attention to detail underlies the quest for an exploration of the text, which, in his surrounding theatrical world of contemporary Moscow, was rarely encountered. One is aware of the soul of an erstwhile musician, ensuring that the young actors and directors, display the same care in preparation which instrumentalists and conductors devote to their performance.

'It is up to the actor to compose the music of his feelings to the text of his part and learn how to sing those feelings in words. When we hear the melody of a living soul we then, and only then, can come to a full appreciation of the worth and beauty of the lines and of all that they hold concealed'.[6]

Stanislavsky also bows to the word of the playwright as 'the most powerful source of stimulation' for the actor. Within the text lies the 'super-objective of the plot' and anything outside this will be superfluous to the energy, integrity and art of the performance. Actors must employ all their skill and intelligence to accomplish the main purpose of the dramaturgy, and their 'through line of action' leading to the 'super objective' must be so focussed as to make inspiration possible by 'preparing a favourable ground for it'.[7]

He acknowledges the presence of the audience – 'the spiritual acoustics for actors' – and yet at the same time he refutes the actor's need to embrace them in a demonstrative way: actors must have a point of attention and this attention must not be the auditorium. The actor must focus upon and within a series of 'circles' of concentration which begin with self and end at the stage area. Whilst the audience may be gripped by the skills of the actors creating the illusion of realistic characterisation,

---

[4] Stanislavsky, C. p. 83.   [5] Stanislavsky, C. p. 94.   [6] Stanislavsky, C. p. 115.
[7] Stanislavsky, C. *An Actor Prepares* (Translated by E. R. Hapgood. Theatre Arts Books, New York, 1948) pp. 256–265.

they 'observe' rather than pay court to, displays of the familiar 'look-at-me-the-character-I-am-playing' syndrome.

And yet Stanislavsky is propounding one of the basics of the narrative techniques of acting; that of illustrating what is said in such a way as to recreate the sharpness of the original stimulus: the act of living, or more correctly 're-living' a role or narrative. By acknowledging the audience to stimulate response and counter-response ('action and re-action') this leads to increased inspiration and a refreshed sense of recall, which in turn reaches into the innermost depths of the visual and emotional memory.

Thus Stanislavsky asks his actors to reach into self as the primary source of reference, for the reproduction of feelings and experience, within the reconstituted guise of the character he is playing.

The actor lives within the role: '...never lose yourself on stage. Always act in your own person, as an artist... the soul of a person he portrays will be a combination of the living elements of his own being'[8]

The training of the actor therefore is predominantly concerned with the means of drawing upon his emotional resource material, so that he may discover methods of creating 'an infinite number of combinations of human souls, characters, feelings, passions for your parts'.[9]

Stanislavky's main philosophical development was – in part – a reaction against the principles of exaggerated, declamatory acting currently on display in most European theatres. The basis of his theories was gathered also from his own considerable experience as an actor and director, within this contemporary theatrical climate.

What is so surprising and exciting to me when I re-read the writings of Stanislavsky, is the freshness and modernity of his 'methodology', especially when considered alongside the present climate of European actor-training. What he proposes so carefully, is a philosophy of preparation which has a daily routine of exercise, and which parallels the intensity of preparation and commitment, associated with the musician or dancer.

Within the context of the complex, contemporary scientific theories of reflexology, feelings and memory, as proferred by such scholars as Pavlov, Theodule Ribot, Ivan Sechenov, his quest is so clear and so logical.

Firstly, to evolve a system which creates the potential for truth.

'Everything which happens on the stage must be convincing to the actor himself, to his associates and to the spectators. It must inspire belief in the possibility, in real life, of emotions analogous to those being experienced on the stage by the actor. Each and every moment must be

---

[8] Stanislavsky, C. pp. 167–168.   [9] Stanislavsky, C. p. 168.

saturated with a belief in the truthfulness of the emotion felt, and in the action carried out by the actor'.[10]

Secondly, to solve the perennial problem for the theatre, by creating 'an inner life for a play and its characters, to express in physical and dramatic terms the fundamental core, the idea which impelled the writer, the poet, to produce his composition'.[11]

Thirdly, to devise a system of training for the actor, based upon the 'laws of nature' which is a whole way of life'... 'so that you can only assimilate it, take it into your blood and flesh, until it becomes second nature, becomes so organic a part of your being that you as an actor are transformed by it for the stage and for all time'.[12]

Stanislavsky describes a philosophy of training from which unfolds the mystery of the player's skill, igniting a profound sense of spontaneity and inspiration, bringing a compulsive dynamism to a rehearsed and repeatedly performed role.

In very basic terms the 'rule of thumb' for the actor in his training and in his preparation for his role, is the quest for truth, as created by the writer, employing all the skills and resources available to reveal that truth by the actor, for himself, and afterwards his audience.

The question of 'truth' and whose truth, is one of the problems of Stanislavsky's objectives. The truth as the actor recalls and relives in his role or the truth as it is revealed and edited by the director, or the truth of both these truths as it is reviewed by the audience?

Whatever the quest for 'truth', the ideal is, that through a rigorous, continuous and unrelenting period of training, the actor maintains a highly tuned, physical and psychic condition. As a result, he is so liberated through habit as to be able to technically read a 'score' with little difficulty, and then, by making reference to his ever-changing living resource, create a performance which is both spontaneously inspirational, familiarly organic, and recognisably 'true' to life.

'Each dramatic and artistic image created on the stage is unique and cannot be repeated, just as in nature... [as in birth]'.[13]

'You should develop your bodies, your voices, your faces, into the best physical instruments of expression capable of rivalling the simple beauty of nature's creations... true creativeness comes from within, from human and not theatrical emotions. It is towards this goal that we should strive'.[14]

---

[10] Stanislavsky, C. p. 122.
[11] Stanislavsky, C. *Building a Character* p. 266.
[12] Stanislavsky, C. p. 290.
[13] Stanislavsky, C. *An Actor Prepares* p. 295.
[14] Stanislavsky, C. *Building a Character* pp. 295–298.

At the end of his life 'Stanislavsky laid down with a definitive sense of finality the premise that all the psychological and emotional complexities of the mind, of the transmission of thoughts and feelings are inextricably represented by physical action. There is always a sense from the very beginning of Stanislavsky's search for the actor's 'truth' that in the theatre *the word is complementary to the action. They are inseparable.*

It is my feeling that there is much of what Stanislavsky proposed that is especially relevant to the needs of the present-day actors. It is significant that in the following account of the work of his successors I refer constantly to other aspects of Stanislavsky's experience and philosophy. It is a measure of my wonder at the timelessness and profound quality of his experience and of the resulting theories of actor-training.

MEYERHOLD, Vsevolod Emilievich (1874–1940)

The basis of the art of theatre is acting... to show life on the stage means to perform life. [15]
The stage is a world of marvels and enchantment, it is breathless joy and strange magic. [16]

If Stanislavsky's ultimate objective was an attempt – within the proscenium – to frame the illusion of reality, where all characters were played by actors trained to utilise their own autobiographical resources, Meyerhold strove – in sharp contrast – to make a three-dimensional stylised view of an ever-changing humanity spill into the lap of the auditorium with 'no effort made to induce the spectator to forget that he is in a theatre' [17] Meyerhold undertook to evolve a style of acting and a theatrical environment which was consistent with this view.

Stanislavsky was to remain a loyal admirer of the theatrical exploration of Meyerhold, whilst rarely subscribing to his philosophy. Although Stanislavsky was Meyerhold's early mentor, it was not long before Meyerhold was decrying the Stanislavsky methodology almost out of hand.

His first major departure was in his attitude to the audience, and how he expected it to respond to the actors. He expected his audiences to

---

[15] Braun, E. *Meyerhold on Theatre* (Translated and edited by E. Braun Methuen, London, 1969) p. 148.

[16] Braun, E. *The Theatre of Meyerhold* (Interview, 24 November 1913. Methuen, London, 1979) p. 5.

[17] Braun, E. *Meyerhold on Theatre* (Translated and edited by E. Braun Methuen, London, 1969) p. 44.

become engaged in the action. He wanted them to mix the Impressionist's palette of suggestion and mystery, by creating a style which would orchestrate innuendoes and pauses and leave gaps within a stylised form, so that the audience made their individual and unique contribution '... a work of art can influence only through the imagination. Therefore it must constantly stir the imagination... it must really stir it; not leave it inactive through trying to show everything'.[18]

Whilst the early methodology of Stanislavsky proposed a triangular conception of the work of author and actor as filtered through to the audience via the director, Meyerhold saw the audience as the final arbiter of the linear creation passed on to them from the original conception of the author, to the director, through the 'soul' of the actor. 'The spectator is made to comprehend the author and the director through the prism of the actor's art'[19] the New Drama must be 'infectious' and must 'intoxicate' and must have an irrepressible dynamic. 'The audience must participate in a corporate creative act'.[20]

It must also extend its boundaries to be able to accommodate with ease the vast canvasses of the classical theatre of the Greeks and Shakespeare in sharp contrast to the existing plethora of the narrow, limiting land-scape, of Stanislavsky. The task then of the director in the stylised theatre of Meyerhold, is to act as an agency between the artistic and technical creativity of author and actor.

'Having assimilated the author's creation, the actor is left alone, face to face with the spectator, and from the friction between these two unadul-terated elements, the actor's creativity and the spectator's imagination, a clear flame is kindled'.[21]

A fresh and vibrant form of impressionistic theatre was being devel-oped by Meyerhold, where the greater the display of stylised artifice, the more positive and powerful the vision of life; the creation in fact of a new kind of objectivity.

In order to continue the development of this style, Meyerhold turned his attention to the space in which the actor inhabits. In this he revealed his global inquisitiveness and his admiration of the architectural simpli-city of the Elizabethans and the Greeks, and the very basic, aesthetic beauty of the Noh form. In his rejection of the extravagant decorative principles of his contemporaries, he eventually abolished scenery al-together.

'The Stylised theatre liberates the actor from all scenery, creating a three-dimensional area in which he can employ natural, sculptural plas-ticity'.[22] Meyerhold had become preoccupied with the movement of the

---

[18] Braun, E. pp. 26–27.   [19] Braun, E. pp. 52–53.   [20] Braun, E. p. 60.
[21] Braun, E. p. 62.   [22] Braun, E. p. 62.

body in space, in a form which was not dissimilar to that of the dancer and choreographer. The stage space therefore '...must be constructed so that the lines of rhythmical expression can stand out distinctly'... [23]

He compared the actor's method to that of the sculptor, where gesture and attitude, inclination and movement, would contain in its execution the 'essence in form and line of a sculptured portrait'. [24] Meryhold is at his most eloquent about his new style when he describes his visual, theatrical pictures as having...

'...a deft mastery of line grouping and costume colour, which when static creates an infinitely stronger impression of movement than the naturalistic theatre... stage movement is achieved not by movement in the lateral sense, but by the disposition of lines and colours which are made to cross and vibrate... all of this anticipates the revival of the dance... the active participation of the spectator. [25]

From 1909 until his death he extended his stage commitment as director and writer by taking on the mantle of teacher and deviser of acting technique. He took much of his inspiration from the theatre of improvisation as he interpreted it from his reconstruction of the techniques employed in the Renaisssance period of the sixteenth and seventeenth century Commedia Dell'Arte. He is quick to point out that the *improvisations of the Commedia Dell'Arte had a firm basis of faultless technique*. [26]

Although he rarely, if ever used the mask in performance as a means to achieve and define a style of acting, the concept of the mask was uppermost in his mind'... is it not the mask which helps the spectator fly away to the land of make-believe?' [27]

'The theatre of the mask has always been a fairground show, and the idea of acting based on the apotheosis of the mask, gesture and movement is indivisible from the idea of the travelling show. Those concerned in reforming the Contemporary theatre, dream of introducing the principles of the fairground booth into the theatre'. [28] He became preoccupied with devising a concept of movement, which for him was more important than any other theatrical element.

The syllabus for the students of acting for his 1916–17 programme included a now-familiar list of exercises which lead to the acquisition of definite physical and vocal skills. What was particularly significant was Meyerhold's inclusion of the conventions of Hindu, Japanese and Chinese theatres in 'Subjects for Discussion and Stage Acting', as well as the expected references to the more immediate traditions of more 'local' European theatre.

---

[23] Braun, E. p. 91.   [24] Braun, E. p. 93.   [25] Braun, E. p. 63.
[26] Braun, E. p. 129.   [27] Braun, E. p. 131.   [28] Braun, E. p. 134.

From Japanese theatre particularly, he was influenced by the meticulous preparation and development of skills which prepared the actors for the physical complexities of the dance. 'Where does the human body, possessing the suppleness of expression demanded by the stage, attain its highest development? In the dance'.[29]

The examination rules were significant and detailed. Candidates were expected to demonstrate a sound proficiency in music, physical agility, mime, diction, the theories of prosody, art from such as painting or poetry, and dramatic history.

In subsequent years he continued to develop the content and range of his courses, including a new and important emphasis upon the designer/director collaboration as well as a system of practical exercise called *'biomechanics'*.

The exercises were compiled from various sources which Meyerhold adapted and re-defined to furnish his own philosophy.

'The actor must train his material (the body), so that it is capable of executing instantaneously those tasks which are dictated externally (by the actor and director)'.[30]

This method of training was similar to that of the dancer whose body and mind were so highly tuned that it was able to respond instantly to the creative demands of a piece of dance repertoire in collaboration with a choreographer. The actor must develop an innate sense of balance and rhythm and so resolve and train his physical state that he is able to 'experience the exitation which communicates itself to gripping the spectator and induces him to share in the actor's performance'.[31]

Meyerhold defined the need for the actor to follow his system of biomechanics quite simply thus 'Since the art of the actor is the art of plastic forms in space, he must study the mechanics of his body.[32]

The *'Programme of Biomechanics'* for acting workshops in 1922 reads like a list of experiments published in a current medical or scientific journal including such topics as 'The human organism as an automative mechanism' ... 'psychological reflexes' and Mechanisation'.

Whilst this reveals the very open and experimental nature of Meyerhold's enquiry into the new theatrical from, it also illustrates his preoccupation with the actor's role being one part of a big theatrical design and concept. This form of 'biomechanical' agility was ideally suited to the stark simplicity of the new elements of utilitarian, multi-purpose, fit-up scaffolding design loosely associated with a new wave of artistic philosophy called 'constructivism', a design creation which was unobtrusive and purely functional.

---

[29] Braun, E. p. 85.   [30] Braun, E. p. 198.   [31] Braun, E. p. 199.
[32] Braun, E. p. 199.

One forms the impression of Meyerhold becoming a kind of indus-trialised 'time and motion' figurehead following, in a scientific sense, the efficiency and effectiveness – in factory terms, – of the actor in his theatre, working for his audience.

At the beginning of his chapter on Biomechanics he compares the work-ethic of the industrialised workforce ('a joyful, vital necessity') with the lifestyle of the actor and his art. To this end he reminds me of my own record of Rab and his brick laying skills demonstrated at the Transport Museum Glasgow and elaborates his observations in the following way, by referring to

'...those movements in work which facilitate the maximum use of work time... If we observe a skilled worker in action, we notice the following in his movements: (1) an absence of superfluous, unproductive movements; (2) rhythm; (3) the correct position of the body's centre of gravity; (4) stability. Movements based on these principals are distinguished by their dance-like quality; a skilled worker at work invariably reminds me of a dancer; thus work borders on art. The spectacle of a man working efficiently affords a positive pleasure. This applies equally to the work of the actor of the future'.[33]

'In art, our constant concern is the organisation of the raw material. Constructivism [constructivist theatre using multi-purpose, functional sets of stark simplicity offering ideal platforms for displays of Bio-mechanical agility] has forced the artist to become both artist and engineer. Art should be based on scientific principles; the entire creative act should be a creative process. The art of the actor consists in organising his material; that is, in his capacity to utilise correctly his body's means of expression'.[34]

During this period, Meyerhold was also responsible for organising research projects by teachers and students which led to the formation of a 'dramaturgical laboratory' which concerned itself with one of the first serious attempts to evaluate an audience response to a performance. Using this data to 'improve' performance skills, entire productions could be structured to stimulate and exploit audience reaction, confounding its expectations as often as it confirmed them.

It is significant that the State Experimental Theatre Workshop – of which he was the original director – provided a prospectus of training that was subsequently adopted by all the other emerging State Schools.

In 1906 George Fuchs had published a long detailed article entitled 'The Stage of the Future'. This made a deep impression upon Meyerhold at the time. Before his untimely death, whilst imprisoned during the early

---

[33] Braun, E. pp. 197–198.   [34] Braun, E. *Meyerhold on Theatre* pp. 198–199.

1940's, Meyerhold had worked tirelessly to develop a theatrical concept which Fuchs would have applauded.

In general terms he described the restoration of the theatre as a festive ritual, involving performers and spectators alike in a common experience which would reveal the universal significance of their personal existence.

More specifically, when the actor 'lifts the mask of the character to reveal his true nature to the spectator he does not merely speak the lines furnished by the dramatist he uncovers the roots from which the lines have sprung'.[35] He does this by re-examining his technique so that he 'utilises correctly his body's means of expression'.[36]

GROTOWSKI, Jerzy (1933–)

'The actor makes a total gift of himself.'[37]
'We can thus define the theatre as "what takes place between spectator and actor".'[38]

Grotowski felt that the audience should be physically at one with the actor so that they can feel each other's physical and psychic presence; what he calls a 'chamber theatre'. This intimacy brings about the removal of the traditional theatrical frontiers, 'in order that the spectator may be stimulated into self-analysis when confronted with the actor'.[39]

The body and mind must be so trained to become liberated from all resistances both physical and mental. To achieve this, the actor has to follow the needs of his art in life. He has to live his art. His art becomes a way of life. He must follow the pattern of training and develop a psychic discipline and physical skills both for self and as part of a collective, relentlessly and unselfishly. He must progress and continue with an almost religious sense of humility.

'Why do we sacrifice so much energy to our art? ... To fill the emptiness in us... Art is a ripening, an evolution, an uplifting enables us to emerge from darkness in to a blaze of light'.[40]

Grotowski believed quite early on what his predecessors had already declared, that it seemed essential that actors (like their counterparts in the world of music and dance) should carefully, thoroughly and timelessly be trained and that this training should begin before the age of fourteen, should last for at least eight years, and should be a continuous source of reference throughout an actor's working life.

---

[35] Braun, E. p. 206.   [36] Braun, E. p. 198.
[37] Grotowski, J. *Towards a Poor Theatre* (Methuen, 1969) p. 16.
[38] Grotowski, J. p. 32.   [39] Grotowski, J. p. 42.   [40] Grotowski, J. p. 212.

Each school should reflect in its discourse and character 'all human behaviour which has made an impression upon us' and should ideally reflect the fact that 'The performance is national because it is a sincere and absolute search into our historical ego; it is realistic because it is an excess of the truth; it is social because it is a challenge to the social being, the spectator'.[41]

Once again the element of 'spontaneity' arises and once again another nuance impinges itself upon the definition. And yet there is a close affinity between Meyerhold's version and that of Grotowski... 'spontaneity and discipline, far from weakening each other, mutually reinforce themselves; that what is elementary feeds what is constructed and vice versa, to become the real source of a kind of acting that glows'.[42]

Grotowski describes the timelessness concerning the never-ending nature of learning and discovery upon which all artists feed. 'I do not put on a play in order to teach others what I already know. It is after the production is completed and not before that I am wiser. Any method which does not itself reach out into the unknown is a bad method'.[43]

When he reflects upon the actor in performance, trained to encounter his audience to share a form of therapeutic exchange, he describes 'this act of total unveiling of one's being becomes a gift of the self which borders on the transgression of the barriers of love. I call this the total act. If the actor performs in such a way, he becomes a kind of provocation for the spectator'.[44]

In the years 1959–1966, under the direction of Grotowski at the Theatre Laboratory, the actor's training exercises were specifically geared towards the elimination of 'resistances and obstacles which hinder him in his creative task... he must know what not to do'.[45]

However, as part of this 'unlearning' process, many familiar and not so familiar exercises had to be experienced so that the actor's basic technical facility could be developed: exercises which he repeatedly refers to as being 'plastic', 'organic', 'resonating', 'respiratory', 'anatomical' and 'sensual'.

In summarising the most important elements of his techniques, Grotowski begins: 'The body must work first. Afterwards comes the voice... if you think, you must think with your body. However it is better not to think but to act, to take risks... if it [the performance] grows spontaneously and organically, like live impulses, finally mastered, it will always be beautiful–far more beautiful than any amount of calculated results put together'.[46]

---

[41] Grotowski, J. pp. 52–53.   [42] Grotowski, J. p. 89.   [43] Grotowski, J. p. 98.
[44] Grotowski, J. p. 99.   [45] Grotowski, J. p. 101.   [46] Grotowski, J. p. 172.

This presupposes that the actor acts as agent between the two opposites of discipline and spontaneity. Whilst spontaneity implies a style both relaxed and casual, there is no sense of lack of discipline in Grotowski's scheme of things. Discipline and spontaneity are in fact, the two complementary aspects of the creative process. (This, I think, has been said before!)

Grotowski refers to an acting 'score', his route of exploration between character and audience, having evolved and been shaped as a result of a long and 'steeping' collaboration between the actor and the director, so that the score is both 'fixed' and 'fluid'. The audience in turn, in its unique, assembled, corporate and individual form, shares with the actor his encounter, his personal enquiry of the role he is experiencing. Questions and replies; the 'give and take' of human contact; like the musician with his 'score' his encounter with it is always slightly different as he opens himself to the new potential of the new audience.

This I think is what Grotowski is referring to when he says that whatever the form of actor's training, his search for discipline and structure is as inevitable as a search for spontaneity. The actor, when encountering the audience has to be in such a refined disciplined state of physical and psychic agility that he is able to open up his character in an original way, and temper his 'performance' to the needs of each individual audience. A perfect host.

Once again Grotowski reminds us of his version of a kind of 'body-life' a version of 'body-memory'; what we touch and what we do, and how we become engaged in 'tactile' experiences with others. He implies that if an actor is fully open to this process, there is released from within his being, an impulse which is fixed as an association, or a physical action. This process can only happen in a living relationship to something else... and with someone else.

Another element of theatre research undertaken at the Laboratory was the nature of the spacial aspects which embrace actor and audience; one in which 'the performance results from an integration of two ensembles'.[47]

In collaboration with the architect Jerzy Gurawski, Grotowski placed his audience close to the action, often integrating them within it. A real extension and development of the theories of Meyerhold. Their collaboration realises some fascinating designs.

For his production of *Dr. Faustus*, the audience sit at long tables as though sharing a feast; the meal served being Faustus' last supper given to his friends; the trestle table tops being the 'stage' area in which this ritual is 'enacted'. In *The Constant Prince* the spectators look down upon the action as though viewing a sporting arena. In *Kordian* the spectators are subjected to the immediate proximity of a ward of an asylum.

---

[47] Grotowski, J. p. 125.

In all cases the design has been developed, within the basic laboratory space and has been moulded around the needs of the play, the action and anticipated reaction of the spectators who are placed carefully within it.

It is fascinating to encounter a theory of theatre and its execution by actors for audiences which argue that words 'in the form of the text, is only a means to release the action'. Grotowski continues by describing this action as 'a fleshing out of words... words must never be illustrated... the spectator likes easy truths. But we are not there to please or pander to the spectator. We are there to tell the truth'.[48]

I find that there is much to reflect upon in the theories expounded by Grotowski, but I find them an unnecessary and often confusing variation on a theme made familiar by this predecessors.

His emptying of the space of the creative mind is based upon the meditative theories of eastern philosophy. As a Quaker I understand the process of wiping clean the cluttered and obstructive inner reaches of the mind so that something spiritual can enter spontaneously, to inspire, to embrace, to reflect upon. Even though, in his preface to *Towards Poor Theatre*, Peter Brook refers to Grotowski's work as 'unique' and a 'model of artistic dedication, monastic and total... a daily challenge'... there is a strong feeling that this has been done before.

There has been conspicuous silence for the past fifteen or so years from Grotowski himself. It is this silence which leads me to suppose that his theories are theories only: whilst they have been tested in 'laboratory' conditions they have not been properly taken up and tested in public theatres. Perhaps the reason has little to do with the theories, and more to do with the present spiritual poverty in theatre. Whatever the reason, as I read and invest my thoughts and instinctive evaluation of Grotowski's work I feel uncomfortable. I am aware of 'words' rather than 'action'.

I am puzzled as to why Grotowski has not continued to follow his passion, to chase his doubts and to create new and stimulating ways in which actors can develop their art. By now, even in the hands of his Polish compatriots, his ideas have become fossilised, and subject to cliché. And yet in Britain, the nature of his exploration, in the mainstream of theatre is almost totally ignored; with the exception of Peter Brook.

BROOK, Peter (1925–)

Whereas Grotowski leaves a deep trough of introspection '... a solitary man playing out his drama alone', Brook the showman travels, 'the opposite way, leading out of loneliness, to a perception that is heightened because it is shared'.[49]

---

[48] Grotowski, J. pp. 193–195.   [49] Brook, P. *The Shifting Point* (Methuen, 1988) p. 41.

Brook's quest is as much devoted to the compulsive need to understand audience, as it is to find a way in which actors can prepare and share their art, so that they can offer a view of life within the celebration of a theatrical event.

The 'Empty Space' of his early career has continued to grow and its shape has changed, but there is a feeling that it has become more fixed than it used to be: more like the snail and its shell; a specifically designed home within which a clearly defined lifestyle has been 'gathered', and one which travels and is sometimes shared.

Brook is a man of considerable theatrical experience. Whilst he has been, and continues experimenting with the challenge of theatrical event as director, he has devoted more than two decades of his considerable career to theatrical experiment.

Le Centre International de Recherche Theatrale (C.I.R.T.) in 1970 provided him with the opportunity to share a period of travel and theatrical experimentation with actors and other directors; a 'journey out'. Almost four years later, in 1974, at the Bouffes du Nord in Paris, he found a more permanent home for theatrical performances – newly named 'Le Centre International de Créations Théatrales' (C.I.C.T.) which included and displayed the period of 'gathering' which had preceded it.

The theatrical process of Brook is deceptively simple. He describes it as having two distinct stages.

'First: preparation, second: birth.'[50]

The first stage is of indeterminate length, depending upon the form and complexity of the theatrical event, and of the inspired way – or otherwise – in which its conception and 'preparation' evolves.

The second stage, is that moment when the performer uses all his 'preparation' resources to enable him to embrace the exacting challenge of each unique audience and the event itself: to re-discover, stage by stage, the shared moments of creation – spontaneous in their revelation, yet composed in form and content – of an erstwhile, almost hidden use of detailed exploration and training.

Brook doesn't 'train' actors. Rather he shares a 'space' with them and becomes engaged upon a mutually committed journey of discovery. He assumes that they bring to this shared experience, their own individual and cultural acting resource, as he brings his own theatrical knowledge of directing and producing. He is not so much a teacher as an editor. He collates and reshuffles the material he assembles with his actors and designers, and then prepares and presents the consequence of the expression of this material, for a further 'sharing' with audience.

---

[50] Brook, P. p. 7.

The time in which he takes to complete this process is determined by the practical and artistic needs of each piece. It changes as the experience of playing in different arenas, before different audiences, in different languages, imposes a re-thinking of emphasis.

The Ik, The Conference of the Birds, The Mahabharata, all produced initially for public scrutiny at the Bouffes Du Nord, reflect and respond to a different time scale of research and discovery, most of which was undertaken during the many years which preceded their public exposure.

The Ik emerged from the group's exploration through improvisation of passages form Graham Turnbull's anthropological studies of a tribe described in his book 'The Mountain People'. The paradox here was that the improvisations were controlled. The physical attitudes of the starving tribespeople in the Ik family were captured in exacting detail, and then fixed so that the narrative could be developed around them.

Such was the conviction of their performance that Turnbull became deeply affected and changed his views on the inhumanity he judged the Ik to be capable of; from one of disgust to compassion. For Brook, this was a fundamental break-through that had taken place as a result of the techniques employed by the actors to discover and 'understand the links that exist between the truth of a form and the quality of what the audience receives'.[51]

> *'Compassion returned. Why? I think this touches on the core of what acting is about. No actor can look at the character he's playing as a cool observer, he has to feel him from the inside, like a hand in a glove, and if he once lets judgement in, he loses his way. In the theatre, an actor defends his character and the audience goes along with him. Our actors had come to be the Ik and thus to love the Ik: and Colin Turnbull, as he watched, found himself transported out of his trained professional stance of observer into something anthropologically suspect, but so normal in the theatre – understanding through identification'.*[52]

The Conference of the Birds was tried and tested in many global locations, but none more challenging than in Africa. Whilst the Africans were often much bemused by the group's often disastrous attempts to test their narrative skills on the 'unrolled mat', the actors and Brook were examining the precise nature of 'Audience'; of how it was constituted: when in time, and in what space it assembled and responded, and how sentiment and preconceptions, preparation and spontaneity, were considered, used, measured,reflected upon, analysed and often feared. It was a time to learn

---

[51] Brook, P. p. 154.   [52] Brook, P. p. 137.

and absorb; to raise countless questions about the nature of the act of sharing a 'performance' with an audience.

He has much to say about acting; about the nature of the Actor's art and what he contributes to the theatrical event.

> *'There is a golden rule. The actor must never forget that the play is greater than himself. If he thinks he can grasp the play, he will cut it down to his own size. If, however, he respects its mystery – and consequently that of the character he is playing – as being always just beyond his grasp, he will recognise that his 'feelings' are a very treacherous guide'.*[53]

Brook continues by demanding that the actor respects the 'form' or 'movement' or the text. He suggests that in order to capture this 'movement' he explores the 'very strange relation between what is in the words of a text and what lies between the words'.[54]

The epitome of the 'form', for Brook is Shakespeare, who 'seems better in performance than anyone else because he gives us more, moment for moment' for our money. This is due to his genius, but also to his technique'.[55]

> *'The strength and the miracle of Shakespearean texts lie in the fact that they present man simultaneously in all his aspects... because deep roots are sunk beyond the everyday, poetic language and a ritualistic use of rhythm show us those aspects of life which are not visible on the surface'.*[56]
>
> *'He reminds us where we are, and thus brings us back to the solid and familiar world where, when all is said and done, a spade is a spade'.*[57]

And my favourite quote 'Shakespeare is a piece of coal that is inert'.[58] When arranged upon the kindling and paper and lit, it 'relives its virtue' and establishes the heart of the fire emitting heat and energy.

Having seen a number of productions directed by Brook in film and theatre, I am aware of a change in attitude, particularly to the actor – at least in theory. In his early career he 'directed' almost exclusively within a tradition of a parochial, western repertoire, presented by actors and designers who displayed their work in theatre spaces which were part of the intrinsic personality of that repertoire.

Whilst he definitely 'directs' in the traditional sense of being the final decision-maker of all the artistic elements, and is unrelenting in his enquiry of an actor's deeply lodged resources, in his latest work, he appears to have made a direct and very crucial decision to explore the parameters of a global theatre having a basic narrative style, which embraces the boundaries and restrictions of communication common to all peoples and all cultures – at least in theory.

---

[53] Brook, P. p. 16.   [54] Brook, P. p. 16.   [55] Brook, P. p. 47.
[56] Brook, P. p. 57.   [57] Brook, P. p. 58.   [58] Brook, P. p. 96.

In terms of the 'space' in which his theatre is housed, he is consistent enough. The inner, circus orchestra, and opened walls acting as a backcloth 'skene', (a version of the open space of Le Bouffes du Nord) is transported wherever the company is playing, whether in the lap of a quarry or the disembowelled interior of a Victorian tramshed. Brook has always been consistent about the arena in which the performance takes place. It must never be 'boring' (in the sense that the texture of earth, water or brickwork can never be boring.) It must be so designed as to offer the actors the opportunity for them to be seen, heard, focussed upon, and enveloped in audience rather than separated from it.

The simple 'narrative' carpets of Africa become the interiors and exteriors of the epic *Mahabharata*. Stepping on and off them is as significant as instantly changing from the Games Room of a palace to the fringes of an oasis.

Despite the fact that Brook's company have brought with them an extraordinary range of training from a wide variety of cultural traditions, the overall impression of their combined style is one which is familiarly western. And when Brook refers to the mysterious 'presence' possessed by so few performers he is equally traditional.

'If I had a drama school,' says Brook, 'I would search for... that quality which makes one actor standing motionless on stage rivet our attention while another does not interest us at all'.[59]

He continues to search with his very open mind. But he has already closed one approach.

In his chapter entitled 'The Mask – Coming Out of our Shell' from his book *The Shifting Point*, Brook on the one hand 'loathes masks in the theatre'[60] and yet in this account of his work on *The Conference of the Birds* he makes many comments about the fundamental effect upon actors wearing mask for the first time. He has much to say about the frozen quality of the mask and its apparent immobility and constrictions, though he concedes that when it is worn by an actor, it is only then that through the mask and its wearer the 'character' seems to have an endless potential of movement and psyche.

Irrespective of the design of the mask – whether it is typical of the cubist masks of Picasso, or a ritualistic mask of the Yoruba – if it is 'worn by a person sensitive to its nature, it has a capacity to express the human condition beyond the experience of the actor... if the human being inside (the mask) is sensitive to its meaning, it has an absolutely inexhaustible quantity of expressions... and the awakening of body awareness is immediately there with it, irresistibly'.[61]

---

[59] Brook, P. pp. 231 232.   [60] Brook, P. p. 223.   [61] Brook, P. p. 219.

He suggests that the unmasked face is such a natural focus for the display of expression, the actor automatically courts its versatility at the expense of the rest of the body. An actor wearing a mask 'can't fail to be instantly aware of everything he normally forgets, because all the attention has been released from this great magnet up top'.[62]

This of course is one of the main elements of my argument that to remobilise the face of the mask, the rest of the body – as an elaborate visual aid – has to be activated.

I am aware that in Brook's company there is a Balinese actor whose displays consummate skill with the masks of his country. He has a very highly developed technique which belongs to a whole tradition of masked training; the same also with an actor trained in Noh. And yet Brook has used these resources only occasionally, which is especially puzzling given his insatiable appetite for pushing aside the western barriers of complacency which seems to harness in such a limiting way our western theatrical style. Perhaps the answer lies in his 'loathing'.

In this same chapter he anticipates with apprehension the use of mask in the production of *The Mahabharata*. In the production itself only one mask was used; an elephant mask worn by the actor Bruce Myers playing the part of the scribe Ganesha, the bringer of peace. It wasn't 'used' at all in the sense that it produced in the actor movements which complemented its design. It simply served to illustrate what it looked like; an elephant's head upon the body of a human; the character as described in the fable. So the mask was used to provide a simple 'environment' within which more exotic and god-like speeches emerged.

Brook's is not alone in his apprehension regarding the use of mask. And here lies one of the major problems; that of the suspicion and lack of belief in the possibility and need to train actors in a western culture to use mask.

If a director like Brook with his artistic openness 'loathes' mask because as he says 'what better instrument do we have than the actor's face?',[63] and continues in his work to perpetuate his anti-mask feelings, then the lesser-known artists in the West, without Brook's resources, will take note of this and be less inclined to focus the training of the rest of the body as a potential acting resource.

That isn't to say that the western theatrical profession as a whole is continually watching and responding to Brook's experiments as though he were a kind of theatrical Guru, but he is noticed, highly respected, and exerts considerable stylistic and methodological influence.

Despite few recent exceptions such as The Swan at Stratford and the Royal Exchange at Manchester, British theatres remain large and alienating.

---

[62] Brook, P. p. 219.   [63] Brook, P. p. 219.

They are designed to accommodate the size of audience which will anticipate a suitable production profit... and they have followed a tradition in design based upon the needs of more declamatory Victorian semiotics.

Thus there is an inherent theatre design problem which acts against the actor, whose training prepares him not only for the stage but also for the more 'close-up' needs of film and video. I refer to this in my conclusion.

However, at this point, it is relevant to note that the experimental nature of the work of the four 'directors' briefly summarised in this chapter, led them to similar conclusion about the nature of the task facing the actor in training and can be summarised succinctly by Brook in chapter nine of *The Shifting Point*, entitled 'Entering Another World'. He describes a view of 'another world' of training and philosophy which is almost completely alien in length and concept to, for instance, our present actor-training establishment in Britain.

> *'He [the actor] has to serve the embodiment of a human image that is greater than what he thinks he knows. Therefore he has to put into service highly prepared faculties. And that's why an actor has to train and keep on training. A musician has to do this daily with his hands, his ears and his brain, a dancer has to do it with whole of his body; but an actor has to put even more of himself into play. This isn't what makes—or rather, could make—acting the supreme art. Nothing can be left out. The supreme actor is imitating the supreme man. Therefore he has to have available every faculty that can belong to a human being. This of course is impossible, but if the challenge is recognised, the inspiration and the energy will follow.'* [64]

It is to this challenge that I now address my enquiry.

---

[64] Brook, P. pp. 233–234.

2
ACTOR-TRAINING

Actor-training: An Alternative

Whilst I use the resources assembled in the body of the next three volumes to support the findings of my philosophy, it is important to state that mine is a totally subjective view.

The tone of disquiet, which I used in my introduction, remains with me. I make no apology for this. It is one thing to challenge negatively what exists at the present time, and another to offer positive practical suggestions which effect change, and hopefully, improvement.

My purpose has been to investigate a way in which – by reason of training – the actor can stand alongside other performance artists such as musicians and dancers and be acknowledged as possessing performance skills which are recognisably professional, and are commensurate with that professional sense of being part of a way of life.

It is my contention that there is an important dimension of an actor's training in Britain which is largely ignored; it is the *physical* language of performance.

Our theatres are filled with plays which reflect an oral tradition, and are sound based. Plays in our theatres are mostly to be heard and not seen. I suspect that the extraordinary extravagance of the designs which surround these 'orations' are the subconscious product of the need to fill the physical gaps. Those with the ultimate responsibility – the directors – with a few notable exceptions, seem oblivious to the problem.

I am in no way blaming either the training establishments, the actors, or the theatres for this discrepancy. They all are caught up in the game of survival. The main consequence of this is that actors are expected to shift effortlessly between theatre, television, film, sound and video production in order to earn a living at a very basic level. One feeds off the other. A promising actor, fresh from Drama school is 'spotted' and lured into television. A long series or regular appearances in a popular 'Soap', and he will be lured back to the theatre having a newly acquired 'star' status. There are countless sad tales of disappointments and break-downs.

Acting in the theatre is a demanding and a *uniquely* special art. It cannot be developed casually or quickly. It demands a lifetime dedicated to practice and learning.

What I am proposing is not a total revolution which decries all existing theatre and the training for it. However, it is my belief that – with few exceptions – there is a present condition which seems to resist the artistic energising of fresh endeavour and exploration.

This is the time for a new and exciting development, which works alongside the existing theatre genre, draws some inspiration from it, and opens up a vision and awareness of other styles and skills which are available in other performing arts, and those of other cultures: for British Theatre to become more global in its concept, in the same way that music and dance is thus informed.

I have drawn upon the experience of much *practical* experiment, and have examined the Italian Commedia, the Japanese Noh, and the Yoruba Masquerade to support my proposed philosophy. The common factor in all this enquiry is the mask, and the way in which it demands a physical language to animate it.

I have referred briefly to the experiments of Meyerhold, Stanislavsky, Grotowski, and Brook. They are united in the importance they place upon the high level of physical fitness and agility they demand from their actors.

It is this area of physical skills and the resulting awareness of the presentation of a new physical language, that I feel holds the key to solving in part, the missing dimension in our theatre performance.

Current Training Programmes for Actors in British Schools, Colleges and Universities

Intending students of acting are likely to choose their programme of training from one of the Drama Schools included in the Conference of Drama Schools. It was formed 'largely as a means of strengthening the voice of member schools and in order to develop and encourage the highest standards in training for both actors and stage managers.'[1]

In the introduction to its 'Guide to Courses' it lays out its general purpose.

'We have tried to provide a clear and simple description of each school, its policy and the courses it offers. It will not be surprising that there is a good deal of repetition. Work on the voice and the body and a study of the art of

---

[1] Kitson, G. & Jago, R. (Eds.) *Guide to Courses, 1989–1990* (Conference of Drama Schools) p. 4.

acting must lie at the basis of every course in professional training... But in the manner in which these disciplines are taught there is a great deal of variety, far more than we have been able to express. What the schools enjoy in common is the determination to preserve the highest possible standards of professional training'.[2]

Each school member of the 'Conference' is subject to repeated and continuous accreditation procedures which are designed to examine the level of facility, teaching and course programme which prepares for the highest professional standards. The body which administers this is called the National Council of Drama Training (NCDT) and it includes a panel of people selected from the theatrical profession and especially the Equity Union.

'Acting courses and Stage Management courses accredited by the NCDT are indicated at the end of each school's entry.'[3]

For most schools, this accreditation by the profession provides its own status in terms of admissions, and also can be used by the colleges to persuade local sponsors and authorities of the urgent need to finance the provision of 'plant' or teaching facilities which may – in their judgement – be lacking.

Throughout the booklet, there is reference to a variety of approaches which students of acting will encounter during their period of training. *Improvisation* figures largely. There is occasional reference to the theories and techniques of Alexander, Laban, Stanislavsky and in some schools a definite preference in policy which displays a bias towards Europe and musical theatre.

It is very evident from the published accounts of the work of these important organisations that there is no lack of artistic purpose or integrity either in their facilities or their teaching skills or – most importantly – their caring concern for the emotional and artistic development of their students.

However, for the most part there is a feeling that in the end, the training process, has no overall philosophical base other than one which is coincidental. What is provided is a 'real-world' package which indicates the need to know how to rehearse, and how to survive amidst the infinite variety of theatre or media experience currently available – particularly in London.

The detailed 'way of life' use of explorative techniques appropriate to character, repertoire, and the artistic style of the production in performance, is buried under a three week rehearsal tradition in the theatre, or

---

[2] Kitson, G. & Jago, R. p. 5.   [3] Kitson, G. & Jago, R. p. 4.

a cut-throat, 'time-means-money' deadline of studio booking or location availability.

What is generally regarded as being normal working conditions in British theatre is that there is little time to do anything other than learn lines, entrances, exits, and the basic geography of the design. Anything beyond that is unusual and considered a luxury; almost a perverse extravagance.

There are very few groups of actors in theatres in Britain, who enjoy the time and space to unhurriedly and thoroughly develop their skills and explore their art, in the same way that Brook's International Centre of Theatre Research operates at the Bouffes du Nord in Paris. It is perhaps relevant at this point to digress and look again at the original purpose of this experiment which began in 1970.

> 'The people were actors from all over the world. The Centre was a point where different cultures could converge... Our first principle, we decided, was to make culture, in the sense of culture that turns milk into yoghurt – we aimed to create a nucleus of actors who could later bring ferment to any wider group with whom they worked. In this way, we hoped that the special privileged conditions we were making for a small number of people could eventually enter into the theatre's mainstream'.[4]

There is the inspirational sense in which the commonplace is converted to thinking and moving to a richer form, and that by example, the 'privileged conditions' of working are deemed necessary, fundamental and – in consequence – become commonplace.

In Britain, most performances don't progress artistically beyond the first 'books down run-through' stage. This is not a cynical appraisal but an unfortunate reality. The schools in their wisdom prepare their students for this dulling fact of life. There is little general encouragement to alter the status quo.

Another reason why there is no outcry for change is that audiences in general accept the present state of theatre and continue to support it. Whether they continue to be enriched or not by the 'art' that they see, or whether they have the same expectancy of enrichment as they would if they were offered a staple diet of Brook training and philosophy, is another matter.

Here lies the familiar paradox – the dilemma. If audiences are happy with their lot, why encourage change?

In my view, the boundaries of an audience's experience needs to be constantly challenged if the art is to reflect its social and historical context, and – in consequence – to reconstruct its form and style to accommodate these changes. Theatre has to grow, and the techniques employed by its

---

[4] Brook, P. *The Shifting Point* (Methuen, 1988) pp. 105–106.

professional participants has to match its growth. This is their singular professional responsibility; to challenge and seek the highest standards of creative potential and resist inertia by creating exciting innovation.

For a short time each year the Annual London Mime Festival gathers together innovative companies from all over the world who relfect in their work a more physical approach. *Tag Teatro* from Italy with their distinctive reconstruction of the masked Commedia, *Trestle* in London who explore a more modern multi-media masked theatre form, and more recently *Théâtre de Complicité* exemplify what Kenneth Rea describes as a theatre in which 'bodies started to become important.'[5]

What I propose is a much longer and more exacting process of training, which can co-exist with the current system. This training will be predominantly biased in favour of a more rigorous examination of physical acting skills which will be tested both in the classical repertoire and new works.

Firstly, it must be stated that, in the continuing tradition of western theatre there is no distinction between male and female actors. They are implicitly embraced in the singular term 'actor'. All plays, all parts, all training, must accommodate the sexes equally.

I wonder how many of us would actually like to be able to play a musical instrument proficiently enough to make it worth listening to, and how many of us take the first enthusiastic steps, towards this dream, and fall away almost immediately when confronted with the reality of the repetition of practice, and the learning of skills and technique.

There is however, a process of learning in Dance and Music, which is long established, having a proven philosophical and practical base. The standardised syllabus of training devised and tested by the Royal College of Music and the Royal Academy of Dance is undertaken by thousands of pupils and supervised by hundreds of dedicated and skilful teachers.

Whatever the amount of natural talent or motivation on the part of the pupil, there is a baseline of skill and technique which has to be absorbed totally and demonstrably established, before the artistic interpretation of music or dance can be considered. This base line expands as the degree of difficulty increases. Repertoire is considered according to where on this route the technique has been consolidated. There is a place for this learning included in our schools and in special centres of advanced training in both the public and private sector. This process can begin at a very early age.

---

[5] Rea, K. *The Guardian* (January 17th 1990).

Actor-training: The Beginnings

If we take the example of the Noh, then it should begin officially on the sixth day of the sixth month of the sixth year of life. As I shall describe in the next volume. On the training of Noh actors, the youngest child I saw – who was already some way into his training programme – was three years of age.

In music and dance there are often physical considerations of growth and size, financial and family support, geographical location as well as innate artistic motivation and talent which may have a profound effect upon the development of the young, amateur performer.

Although there is an approximate timescale by which certain stages should have been achieved, students are encouraged as individuals to progress at their own pace. The same considerations will prevail for the actor-beginner. The main thing is that it should begin as soon as possible.

Acting out in play, the games of 'pretend' and mimicry are part of the natural process of learning. There is acting potential in all of us. There lies part of the problem. We all do it in one form or another and think we could do it professionally. There seems to be little to it. We all at sometime or other re-enact our experiences as well as 'act the fool'. Some encourage a more widely acclaimed response to their 'acting out' than others.

There is much educational material offering a resource of ideas and practices which can be used by teachers of drama, taking the beginner through the early stages of drama training, from play to performance. It is not my intention to ignore this existing resource.

The problem lies in the degree to which these beginnings are broken down systematically into logically recognisable layers, which can be best tested in specially prepared performance pieces, at each graded level of progression. This is not to proclaim a new exam system, but a way of measuring the state of absorption of skills, fundamental to acting, for the benefit of teacher and pupil.

If we use the Noh as an example, we remember that each teacher of Noh, has achieved a high level of professional skills before he is allowed to take on the responsibility of passing on those skills. Whilst he is teaching, he is continuing his own learning as a professional Noh player. He is always able to relate to his own role as pupil, and also the reality of his practical application of his learning as a professional. He is ideally placed to instruct; although, as with dance and music, it is not always the best performers who make the finest teachers.

All the work that is learned in Noh is tested in performance from a very young age in plays which contain parts appropriate to the degree of skills acquired. One of the problems with relating this system to western training is that in our system there is just not the repertoire of plays where a wide range of skills learned can be tested in performance.

One of the first needs is to create a systematic programme of learning, and a graded repertoire of dramaturgy which will test that learning in performance.

Plays can include these structured layers of learning, in the same way that ability and experience is accounted for in the developing gradations of music and dance. Playwrights will need to be encouraged to write plays for the beginner and for all those layers of skill which lead up to the highest levels of performance.

In Noh theatre, at all stages of their training irrespective of age, the actors are reaching for the unattainable 'blossoming of the flower,' and are unswerving in their search for it. They also are encouraged in the process to learn from each other in order to find it.

At some stage, this basically amateur state of training is reviewed, and crucial decisions by teachers concerning the student have to be made. If the decision is to go into the acting profession, then a full and proper assessment of the potential of the student as professional actor will have to be made.

At the present time in Britain this stage is the one at which students apply for entry to drama school. At eighteen they are required usually to hold a minimum of academic qualification to qualify for authority funding. Most students have to secure private funding.

So whatever the idiosyncrasies of the establishment and its philosophy, whatever the funding, in general, it is safe to assume that the existing training for the acting profession begins officially at age eighteen.

The expected examination for entry is by audition, the way in which performers are, by and large, selected for their roles in the profession. So whatever their background training in any related performing arts discipline, (or not as the case may be) this is the process by which they are chosen to begin their professional training. It remains woefully inadequate, and usually relies on such nebulous characteristics as personality, physical looks, liveliness, being articulate, a previous dance training, a demonstration to be able to relate to others, and respond to direction in a group workshop. The methods are ad hoc, and form very superficial assessments.

In the Noh, the progression from the Kokata to the position of Uchideshi is natural and comparatively straightforward. By the time the young actor is ready to make a decision to enter into the Noh School and begin his new 'way of life' he has developed to the appropriate level, technical skills in travelling, dance, the use of the fan and props, and will have performed a number of times in festivals of Noh and in Noh cycles with the school he intends to join. He will have been training for at least six years and will be about twelve years of age.

He will already have shared the performing space and the green room for some of these years, being able to observe the many rituals, and be gradually included in their preparation. Thus he will learn by experience and observation, the infinite details of the process of preparation, rehearsal and performance.

Apart from the simple but significant ritual of acceptance, the transition will be almost unnoticeable. There will be no separate test, only an acknowledgement that the early preparation has been thoroughly and successfully completed and that the potential talent for performing has been revealed.

By the time he is eighteen he will have been training for say twelve years, the last six for many hours concentrated practice and learning each day. And yet he will also be encouraged to fulfil all the traditional basic social training and a full primary and secondary education. The pattern is familiar and normal in our own musical and dance establishments.

So why not in acting?

There is no tradition. Whilst there is a plethora of highly trained teachers in Music and Dance, there are very few specialist teachers in acting for young children. There is very little dramatic literature which enables the young child to learn the language of plays and theatre in the same way that there is an abundance of material setting out clearly, schemes of learning which leads to a literacy in music and dance.

One acting resource is exclusively available, though in my view, mainly undesirable. There are voice and speech specialists who offer lessons in elocution. These are usually taught privately, or form part of the curriculum of public schools. In the public sector they are almost non-existent.

Although such teaching has been traditionally associated with the theatre, voice and speech is more to do with losing regional accents in favour of procuring a grammatically correct form of 'received pronunciation'; more to do with the theatre of social soundings and public impressiveness than shaping and placing the voice to embrace an audience in an auditorium.

We have to look at specialists who already help professional actors to prepare their voices, and their speeches, so that sounds and rhythms and emphasis are properly shaped and produced on stage. Such a specialist is Cicely Berry of the Royal Shakespeare Company who has been the voice coach for the company for many years, and for whom the intricacies of speech – especially of the classical playwrights such as Shakespeare and Aeschylus – have been a life study.

There are countless voice specialists who prepare the voices of professional singers. They are mainly concerned with the development and maintenance of the voice of singers of opera and oratorio, who confront as wide a variety of challenge in terms of the repertoire they are expected to perform, as there are composers who write for their instrument. Singers are taught how to shape and place their voice, how to animate it and project it without strain or stress; also how to maintain and protect it from damage.

In complete contrast, this type of voice training is totally alien to the singers of the Chinese Opera. They simply learn their music, and their words, and spend a set amount of time each day projecting both, as forcefully as possible, at a wall.

In similar vein, Paul McCartney, will prepare his voice for a long and arduous tour of public performing by simply 'singing a lot' for a few weeks prior to the tour.

There is a widely held belief that the voice grows in shape and versatility by simply using it a lot in the performance space. Each space requires a different technique. Only by doing it continually will this skill develop.

This is what happens in the Noh. There is never a question of the actors not being understood or heard. The colour and tonal resonance of their voices can be altered to a certain degree, and certain roles lend themselves to a certain timbre. But the method of developing the voice is not set down, it deserves hardly a mention. The skills, whatever they are, are learned from experts, by practicing them as part of a daily ritual, and then continually testing them in rehearsal and performance.

By using these brief examples of existing voice teaching methods, I am trying to show that there is no lack of readily available expertise which can be activated. It is the acknowledgement of the need to harness these skills and expertise which is my primary concern. This expertise and performance opportunity must be made available to all, and become as much part of the training of young actors as it is already well established in music and dance.

I think that I have laboured the Music/Dance analogy enough to take it for granted that it is always in my mind when I am measuring the skills employed by actors.

Conviction

Writers may have certain actors and directors in mind when they are creating their work, but they rarely write with particular acting skills in mind.

I remember putting this question to David Edgar and other contemporary writers who visited the Workshop Theatre at Leeds. In all cases they confessed that actor's skills and their training, 'the nature of the acting animal' was rarely in their thoughts. Certain actors perhaps like Anthony Sher, whose physicality is well known, would expect to have this side of his acting personality accommodated in any script specially written for him. Writers have to be convinced that such a training in physical language is both necessary and artistically stimulating.

Directors and direction are generally under scrutiny and much of the familar debate is explored in the publication *A Better Direction* (1) which records the results of a national enquiry into the training of directors for theatre, film and television.

It is not my intention to offer a detailed criticism of this report. There is much significant commentary about the training of directors which coincided with my own criticism of actor-training. The conclusion of the report offers a significant appraisal of the present state of basic training.

> *As far as training for directors is concerned, there appears to be no one institution that offers a complete vocational training. All that exists at the moment is bits and pieces of training that cannot pretend to go into any serious depth. Some institutions are at present doing the right things, but not doing them well. Some should not be attempting what they are doing because they are not equipped for it, through lack of facilities, staffing or funding.*[6]

The solution to this state of affairs follows.

> *Ideally, what is needed is at least one consistently conceived, thorough training course that will address itself to the full range of skills a theatre director requires at a level equal to the best training abroad. This can only happen in a school that offers training in all departments of theatre because a director cannot train properly without access to actors, designers, stage managers and so on. Until such a course is set up the problem of director training in Britain will never fully be solved.*[7]

If one accepts this information and advice as being close to the truth, then I feel that it is more than coincidence that my research into actor-training methods has appeared alongside it.

However, if a detailed technical training facility is devised, financed and established along the lines recommended in the report, it still doesn't account for a philosophical view.

In the context of this book, and within the philosophy I am proposing, directors will need to be convinced that there is a whole area of an actor's visual, physical facility which is available to him to animate the playwright's intention.

Directors therefore will have to be trained alongside the actors at all stages. In fact it is possible that many directors will emerge from the actor-training programme, as orchestra conductors and choreographers do from theirs, either during their training, or when they are no longer

---

[6] Rea, K. *A Better Direction* (Calouste Gulbenkian Foundation, London 1989/90) p. 156.
[7] Rea, K. p. 156.

able to fulfil the standards required of their profession at the end of their performing career.

It is not as though this philosophy is new to the profession. Implementing it may seem novel, but there is a strong current of opinion, as well as practical evidence, that a physical awareness in performance is beginning to quietly infiltrate the mainstream of British theatre.

A Better Direction was researched and written by Kenneth Rea. Wearing his journalistic mantle, in his survey of the *London Mime Festival*, said that 'physical or visual theatre – washed off the stigma of the white face and thrilled larger audiences with its energy and freshness... On stage, bodies started to become important'.[8]

There is no shortage of representation of this philosophy in high places. Kenneth Rea continues in the same article 'Richard Jones established a strong line in expressionistic productions at the Old Vic, featuring actors from the experimental theatre, while at the National, Stephen Berkoff was invited to do a voluptuous Salomé... and the godfather of new mime, Jacques Lecoq will give workshops on Greek chorus for the National Theatre Company.'[9]

Whilst Kenneth Rea applauds this innovation, he is critical of the artist who in his view has 'become increasingly preoccupied with style over content. Time and time again, the performance work is seductive to the eye but it leaves the brain unengaged'. He wonders if 'audiences eager for the thrill of the new, are too often swindled by the Emperor's new clothes syndrome – intimidated into thinking they should be appreciating something that isn't there. The awful possibility is that, underneath all the flashiness, the new generation of experimentalists may not have anything to say'. He concludes his article by saying that

> *Ironically, the Achilles heel of new mime is the inferior quality of its texts – often devised through informal improvisations. What we now need are playwrights who understand how to write for the body as well as the voice, and directors who can put those two elements together. If we recall Berkoff's plays like East and Greek, and his joyously visceral productions of them, we have a glimmer of the possibilities.*

So there is much evidence that a strong undercurrent of professional preoccupation with physical, visual theatre, exists in British and European theatre. The next question is how to advance the theoretical and physical training of this movement, to consolidate the genre? In my view, through the mask.

---

[8] Rea, K. *The Guardian* (January 17th, 1990).
[9] Ibid.

3

ACTING THROUGH MASK

Hiding the Actor

In my introduction I concurred with Edward Gordon Craig's delibera-
tions on the need to hide the actor's face with the mask, so that 'it compels
him to pay attention to his movements, to rely on his physical means of
expression'.[1] Having explored the masked world of Commedia, Noh and
Masquerade in the ensuing volumes in this series, I am convinced that an
intensive period working in mask is the vital element in the training
programme and physical philosophy which I propose.

In Chapter 1, I referred to Peter Brook's apprehension regarding the use
of mask and also to his comments concerning the fundamental effects
upon actors who wear a mask for the first time.

Brook 'loathes masks in the theatre'[2] and yet at the same time he
acknowledges that

> 'if the human being inside (the mask) is sensitive to its meaning, it has an
> absolutely inexhaustible quantity of expressions... and the awakening of a
> body awareness is immediately there with it'.[3]

The problem is to convince the actor (and his director) of the need to
develop skills which will furnish him with this endless potential of
movement, and that working in mask will not only awaken this potential
but will demand it.

Will it work? Is it worth it? How can this skill be applied and used in
traditional repertoire?

The finest examples of Greek drama were designed exclusively for the
mask. It was continued in Roman theatre and subsequently in the comic
excesses of the Commedia. The masked theatre of the Noh is as influential
and better supported than at any time in its six hundred year history. I
am totally convinced that the current interest in physical and visual
theatre instinctively recalls its masked ancestry. I believe that our training

---

[1] Craig, E. G. *The Mask, The Actor, and The Über-Marionette* (Volume I, 1908–1909,
  Florence).
[2] Brook, P. *The Shifting Point* p. 223.   [3] Brook, P. pp. 218–219.

methods have to respond to these instincts and consolidate its focus upon the re-discovery of the mask despite our lack of indiginous, historical reference to mask in performance, in Britain.

Mask Design

I think all actors should at some time become closely involved with the construction and design of their masks. Supervised by designers and technical advisers, they should 'handle' the fabric of their character at the earliest stage of its evolution, and stay with it, building up its characteristics until its design is consolidated enough to be able wear it, and begin to work from within it.

The Gypsona method (Appendices p. 69) is an interesting technical method which allows instant access to the three-dimensional aspect of the mask and to the psychological elements of character which can be quickly added to the original plaster-casting of the actor's face.

Once the cast has been made, then the designer can determine the general elements of character definition such basic elements as the shape, size and position of the nose and the eyes (see ill. 1). The actor and the designer must, at all stages of its evolution, be making constant checks to the mask, to confirm that the design elements work when it is worn. This facility, of being able to constantly check each stage of the design development is not a luxury, it is crucial to the future progress of the complementary body language of the character.

1. Beginning the gypsona cast

During the process of rehearsal the actor can bring his discovery of the more subtle elements of the character, to the notice of the designer, so that they may be included – or otherwise – in the design of the mask (see ill. 2). This process can be both frustrating and rewarding. It can be extremely difficult to realise a characteristic exactly by remoulding one small part of the mask. In making one alteration, most other elements may need re-adjustment. However, once that detail has been established and fixed, then the actor can begin the long process of learning to animate all the nuances of character.

2. Yuri Dolgikh (Honoured Actor of Russia) working on the features of his mask

In general, the fewer the fixed details, the more enigmatic the potential, and the more versatile the possibilities of the physical effect of the mask in performance. The Ko-omote young woman's mask of the Noh for instance, is perhaps the finest example of a traditional character, so simple in its design, and almost devoid of a clearly defined personality, yet, when worn by a Shite at the height of his acting powers, an extraordinary range of emotions can be released from this mask.

The continuous tactile contact with the mask by the actor, encourages a growing awareness of the psyche of the character, and usually provides a solid base of information. So the first stage of the process is to establish the mask. The more information that the mask includes in its design and the more the actor shares the design process, the greater the potential for the actor to clarify, in his physical presentation, the subtle nuances of character.

Angles and Attitudes

Having established that within the design of the mask lies the elements of character, and that it remains the singular point of reference for the physical, visual aspects of the character it represents, the next stage is to learn to wear it and animate it; to learn to release its spirit in all its 'novelty'

The simple act of donning a mask, seems to motivate the wearer to respond instantly to its abiding spirit. Quite simply, by the very fact that the face is physically covered (and therefore concealed) there is a new focus for the wearer and the onlooker, and the new inanimate face doesn't match the body supporting it. The only way to animate the mask is to discover the essence of its spirit and to activate that spirit through the unique body language which belongs to it.

All bodies have lines, angles, attitudes (see ill. 3). The way a body stands, sits, spreads, folds, tucks, lies, leans, travels, depends upon the individual, his physical condition and natural rhythm, and the infinite cerebral activity which accompanies his personality and actions.

3. Angles and attitudes

In general, a mask uplifted, lightens the state of the character, a mask lowered darkens it. How it moves between and across these two extreme conditions, and at what pace, determines the multiple facets which make up the same personality.

For these facets to work convincingly, each movement has to be accompanied by a complementary physical adjustment. Each placed angle of the mask is matched by a similar signal from hand, arm or leg, or all. In the same way, without the mask, each human body seems to belong uniquely to the face set upon it; not always co-ordinated but recognisable. It is so recognisable and acceptable in fact, we rarely notice it.

Mask operates within a framework. When the mask is 'placed' from side to side (in profile) there is an optimum angle on each side within which the character of the masl remains visible. The same care has to be taken when the mask is elevated (looks up) or dipped (looks down). I call this state of visibility *staying in mask* (see ill. 4).

Once these 'end' positions have been established for each mask then the a framework has been laid down within which the performer knows his character is still visible and active for the audience. Beyond these angles is a condition in which the character disappears. I call this state of invisibility being *out of mask*.

Sometimes a character waiting to enter on can stand in this condition, on the edge of the action, even turning away completely from the audience, and then enters simply by moving *into mask*.

It is not difficult to work out these positions, but it is vital that they are observed at all times. It also has a bearing upon the way in which the movement is choreographed to ensure that performer stays *in mask* when the character is active.

4. Limits of *staying in mask*

The first step for the actor with the mask is to discover the basic rhythms of the new character. These rhythms are to found in the angles and lines and overall shape of the mask. Thus, travelling at different speeds, and shaping the body to accommodate all the basic attitudes needed to stand, sit, lean, stoop, eat, drink, argue, embrace have to be found, learned, fixed, so that they seem familiarly part of the mask.

When the mask is drawn over the head, all these basic movement details and rhythms are embodied also. They must be so learned and finely tuned that the actor, when he is inspired, can be relea sed from them. The mask and the body must be so recognisably in constant harmony, that we accept it and concentrate on other things. The actor as a physical personality must be totally concealed. He must become the living agent for the character he is portraying.

5. Snap-fixing the mask

Two exercises, in the early stages of training, which immediately come to mind are the *snap-fix* and *hand-mask* exercises. What they achieve very quickly is a concentration of focus for the performer; in particular the technical information needed to move the body at any one time, in support of the mask.

Snap-fix Position an arm somewhere in front of you, pause, and snap your fingers at the end of the extended arm. Follow the 'place' of the snap sharply with the mask and focus upon the snap, remaining still for a moment before... positioning the other arm in another position, snapping your fingers focus on the snap, pause... and repeat.

Remember:- arm, snap, look, fix – in that order (see ill. 5).

41

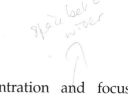

6. Hand and mask exercises

As your concentration and focus sharpens, speed up the sequence, varying the distance between the snaps (and changing the plane) but always pause for a moment to fix the look... and so on. Eventually start to travel with each 'look' so that the legs and feet are consciously brought into the action.

Hand-mask In this exercise one hand begins to move in any direction and in any shape and rhythm and the mask follows it, echoing its shape and rhythm of travel (see ill. 6).

The action is passed from hand to hand and the mask focus follows. The action can pass across and around the body changing shape and height matching the personality of the changing shape of the hand and the way in which it moves.

It is almost inevitable that the rest of the body moves in support of this action. If it doesn't it must be made to do so, so that there is the same conscious link between mask, hands and feet. This exercise can be shared with a partner so that a double-act of interaction develops where one acts as a chorus to the other's protagonist, before reversing roles – and so on.

In mask, all exchanges of dialogue are choreographed in this way, like a piece of dance; the words sitting upon a physical interaction.

It is no accident that the famous terracotta relief in the Lateran Museum in Rome, which is thought to depict Menander in his studio, shows him contemplating his mask.

This is the way of the Noh also. The time spent dressing before the performance in the Mirror Room is the most important. All that has been learned in rehearsal concerning the physical shape of the character is checked with the mask. The mask, the mind and the body become one.

We can simplify the process for the masked performer in three basic stages: contemplation being the first, exploration to animate the mask with the body being the second, and finally creating the illusion of becoming the character depicted within the design of the mask and knowing precisely what is being presented to the audience from behind it.

In reality, only a small part of the essential elements of the physical performance can be thus checked by the masked actor in front of the mirror, because the body is continuously moving out of eye focus. Here lies one of the most difficult aspects of the whole process, and one in which calls into question the trust which must be placed upon the artistic

7. Contemplate, explore, become

integrity of the director; of checking that all the physical signals and patterns of movement of the masked actor match precisely all the elements of character that move and change with the narrative.

Fortunately, the role of the choreographer, and his sacrosanct position as creator and sole arbiter of what pictures and patterns of movement he creates with his dancers, provides a firm precedent for the director in masked theatre. The only problem for the director in western theatre is that only in rare cases is he equipped to share with his actors, a choreographic experience.

It is my view that, just as actors learn the basic elements of dance and movement, so directors have to be trained in the essential groundwork and concepts of choreography. To be able to prepare the actor in rehearsal to send out to the audience the correct physical signals in performance is a crucial element of theatrical production.

This brings me naturally to the question of what is the actor's perception of his mask-based performance? He has to be totally in control of all the external, physical language of the character he is sharing with his audience. From behind his mask he has to be so aware of what he looks like at all times and in complete control of the physical space around it. How he places and moves his body in relation to his mask dominates his training. He cannot shortcut any of the technical elements which combine with his mask to give him this fundamental repertoire of body signals.

If he is to be able to hide within the spirit of his mask, he can only do so having activated – through a programme of rigorous and continual training – a method of finding an appropriate, idiosyncratic framework of physical language, which complements each mask.

In order that this can be accomplished, it is my view that a programme of physical training – which may include dance, gymnastics, juggling, yoga – is supported by experts, who apply and monitor the states of physical development, the psychology of performance focus, and the accompanying provision of massage and physiotherapy. I want the acting profession to have access to all that vast resource of sport training and analysis, and the medical expertise which supports it.

The actor's body has to be as honed and supple as a dancers' so that he can have complete control over it, and bring to his rehearsal and performance a physical state of preparedness which enables him to create the necessary shapes, patterns and rhythms that are inspired by the role he is portraying.

Rhythm, Rhyme and Reason

Shapes, patterns and rhythms are inherent in the text. The design of the mask is discovered in the text. Within the text lies the clues to character and narrative, situation and plot. Sometimes these fundamental elements which determine the form of the play are explicit, others have to be teased out during the period of research and rehearsal.

Occasionally, there are nuances of action and characterisation which even the playwright is unaware, but is discovered during the rehearsal process and subsequently during performance by the actor.

This is a familiar fact which all actors and directors acknowledge. However, in the process of mask performance which I am proposing, this condition of physical awareness, and the skills required to present it in performance, is considerably heightened.

In response to the declared written rhythms of speech and action of character, the actor has to firstly be aware of these rhythms, and then find the means to disclose them with his voice and his body.

Just as the text is grammatically structured to show clearly the patterns and rhythms of speech, and is technically punctuated to clarify them, so the actor has to punctuate his physical performance with a similar code of developing technical keys. A script then becomes more closely recognisable as a kind of musical score, where the words are matched line by line with a similar notation describing their physical condition and presentation.

What this means in performance is that an actor reveals the interpretation of his dialogue through a continuing stream of rhythmical, physical keys; each key being triggered by its logical, sequential need to complement the word. It is the physical keys which are usually remembered first and which inspires 'in its novelty' the true representation of the dialogue. Animating a mask helps the actor to understand this process.

If this were to be graphically represented on the pages of text, at first glance it would appear to fragment its structure and thus clumsily introduce a slowing-down effect at the expense of 'naturalness' in performance. It is vitally important to break down the complementary elements of action and speech and declare them more slowly, so that they can be more easily assimilated.

This does not mean that each word is presented physically, recalling the melodramatic stylised performances of the Victorian theatre, where gestures were extravagantly posed and postulated.

In music, the technicalities of physically producing the right notes, should be so submerged as to be almost invisible. What is heard is the music not the means by which it is achieved. Likewise with dance. The sequence of moving, interacting, human sculptures which respond to the sound impulse, should not be impeded in effect by an awareness of the physical techniques which create them. It should seem effortless.

Just so with acting in mask. Only the character should be seen and heard. The means to produce that effect should be invisible and appear work-free.

The actor has to be trained to be inquisitive enough to search for and determine physical keys which point and heighten the meaning of language so that each key flows in sequence to the next smoothly and invisibly. This is only possible through being exposed on a daily basis to a repertoire of material which exemplifies this challenge and tests his physical and vocal armoury, and also his ability to interpret the degree of mental complexity demanded by the characters he portrays.

The material therefore must be graded according to each stage of development and training. New material needs to be specially written, and existing texts identified which already have an inbuilt structure demanding specific physical and vocal skills at specific stages of the actor's training and development – a grading of texts according to the skills required to interpret them in performance.

To a certain extent, text and character analysis is a more familiar aspect of drama training in Britain. What is not so familiar is the physical attitudes which go with it; the doing of it.

Pulling the Strings

Puppetry provides another way of helping an actor to externalise an awareness of what a character is doing; and exemplifies the vital importance of precise movement.

Puppets are often described as being 'almost human' in the hands of a highly skilled puppeteer. They can also do many things which are beyond the capabilities of humans. They can fly and jump and contort to such an extent that they become *super*-human. Of course this is never so and is surprising given the approximate technology of their construction. What happens in performance is that the puppet's 'human' movement credibility is assisted considerably by the imagination of the onlooker.

It is my contention that an essential element in the training of actors is for them to have a continuing experience and reference to the workings of puppets. By working a rod puppet or marionette – for instance – the actor has not only to be aware of how to animate it, but also how to work *through* it (see ill. 8).

8. Pulling the strings – acting through

By having the puppet before him, he has to know exactly what technical means produces the correct animation. Vocally he has to focus his attention through this animation. Any slight lack of concentration or precision, which breaks the simultaneous interaction between these two elements, immediately dissolves the credibility of the puppet character. It is a singularly vital lesson.

The puppeteer works technically outside the character of the puppet, but also through it. Similarly, the actor has to use the same sense of 'outsideness' to prepare the technicalities of his physical and vocal keys. He has to know what his audience is seeing as well as what they are hearing. If he, as actor, is seen, then he has lifted his mask – and loses credibility.

Shaping and Sharing the Voice

To truly grasp the deep principles of the chant, one must first master the fundamentals of exhalation and inhalation, train the voice, learn to colour the melodies, and thus arrive at immovable heights of an art founded on a mastery of the breath.[4]

---

[4] Zeami, F. M. *On the Art of Noh Drama. The Major Treatises* (Translated by J. Thomas Rimer and Yamazaki Masakazu. Princeton University Press, 1984) p. 204.

If I seem preoccupied with physical language, it is because I think that it is in this area that our training is particularly lacking. Western actors in general don't know what to do with their bodies, how to train them or use them in performance.

However, there is much expertise in training the voice. We have, in Britain, direct access to some of the best voice specialists available in the West. It is not my contention at this juncture therefore to repeat what is already known. The actor has to be able to develop a voice which is appropriate to the role he is playing and the auditorium in which he is performing. He has to be able to shape and place it according to the acoustic and scale of the performance space.

There are a number of training establishments in Britain who share their voice-training tutors for singers and actors alike. The process of training the voice is designed to create a physical resource of notes, shapes, textures, and breathing techniques which can be referred to and applied to each role being prepared for performance. Actors rarely use this facility when they leave their place of training, whereas singers often remain in close contact with their teachers and their philosophy for the rest of their performing careers.

It is worth noting at this juncture that performers at the Peking Opera and the masters of the Noh, will spend time each day singing and chanting familiar repertoire so that by this constant use and very specific reference, their voices will be shaped and developed according to the needs of their unique performance.

The main point is that here is a mine of information from many different cultures showing **how** to train and preserve the voice for performance. A daily ritual of voice exercise, no matter what the method or philosophy, is vital for the vocal well-being of the serious actor.

Health: Honing the Body

I have little time for the Dylan Thomas syndrome. The glamour and alleged romance of the drunken, cigarette-smoking artist, creating self-indulgent havoc I find singularly unimpressive, and professionally self-destructive. If the mind and body are to release from their artistic resource, a career of inspiring, enriching performances, then the minds and bodies of the actor have to be trained, honed, and maintained at the highest possible state of fitness. The acting profession has countless chronicled histories of actors who have destroyed their careers almost as soon as they have begun by reckless self-abuse.

Once again, it is worth recording that there is a vast resource of physical training programmes from which an actor can strengthen and shape his body. Like the voice, this state of fitness and readiness to be able to meet the physical demands of rehearsal, repertoire and perfor-mance, requires a daily programme of exercise in maintaining the physi-cal state of the body as well as a carefully adhered to dietary plan. There must also be a back-up facility of medical care for the healing of injury, and mental and physical stress.

The current medical expertise which supports teams of sportspeople in their preparation for performance, should also be available to actors.

There is so much untapped expertise in conditioning the body and mind which can be applied and modified to meet the needs of the actor. Again, as with voice training, I don't need to elaborate on the resource, only remind that the facility is readily available, and it is wasteful not to use it.

'The potential actor must begin his training at the age of seven, and he must continue training until he is too old to perform. The path of the Noh actor must be one of monastic dedication'.[5]

Constant Reference

Finally, it is vital that the actor retains a constant contact and reference with his training resources which are either in the hands of an individual teacher, a training school, or both.

I return to the sporting analogy and refer to the golfer's swing or the snooker player's cueing arm. When these basic skills are not functioning properly, the whole of the player's game is affected. To be able to return to any semblance of performance level the sportsman compulsively returns to examining and hopefully correcting the basic problem, usually with the help of his teacher and mentor. Until this correction is achieved, the sportsman's performance will not improve.

In all sports, the basics have to be so sound and familiar, that they can be submerged into the subconscious, and remain invisible to the specta-tor. When a sportsman is performing at his exhilarating best, his skills look effortless. The maintenance of these basic sporting skills is fundamental to the performing levels required to sustain competitive professional standards.

Once again, there is nothing new in this. So why shouldn't this be so for the actor? Within the context of this philosophy, the answer is familiar; there is no programme of basic training which remains fundamental to the actor's art in the West.

If the actor prepares his voice, body, and repertoire, and maintains that continuous programme of learning through performing, watching others

---

[5] Zeami, F. M. Foreword (11).

perform, testing his performance against the reaction of his audiences, he must maintain it so that he may continue to develop his skills; at the same time he must be vigilant to ensure that he always retains those fundamental skills which are his baseline of performing reference.

Maintaining and developing the skills of his art must become an unbroken ritual; a way of life. He may then begin to experience the freedom of expression and artistic potential discovered behind the humility of the mask, which Zeami constantly refers to in his treatises.

'After arduous practice, and when all the dust of artistic ostentatiousness has been washed off an actor, he may suddenly find that the inborn quality of grace arrives of itself, as it were'.[6]

Design

There is a powerful lobby of design-orientated theatre in the West. The way in which costly, high-tech design generally dominates the visual conceptions of productions, implies that the actor's art is insufficient in itself to thrill and embrace a sustaining influence upon its audience. By implication also, this insecurity is in the hearts of the playwrights and directors.

In much of London's theatre and in the Provinces at this time, there is a self – perpetuating plethora of design extravagance. In my view, it has a familiar feeling about it which echoes the way in which the glorious, uncomplicated spaces of Greece gave way to the decadent, decorous extravagance accompanying the decline of Rome and its theatre.

The three productions which come to mind which counter this view entirely, and which have played to capacity audiences, and have been universally acclaimed as being examples of the finest theatrical triumphs of the last two decades, have been productions which have been presented in a space, devoid of sets, having minimal properties. Their design focussed entirely upon the artistic intention of the playwright and focussed this intention upon the artistic direction and acting agents of this intent.

I refer specifically to *Macbeth* directed by Trevor Nunn at the studio emptiness of 'The Other Place' at Stratford, with Ian McKellen and Judi Dench, *Mahabharata* directed by Peter Brook at Glasgow, presented on a rectangle of dried clay in a derelict Transport Museum in Glasgow, and all the productions of Noh which I saw in the twenty foot squares of raised cypress in Tokyo and Kyoto.

---

[6] Zeami, F. M. p. 26.

I have no objection in principle to designers, and all the technical expertise which supports their work. What I do object to is the disproportionate amount of attention and financial support they receive at the expense of the quality training the actor needs and the financial security he requires to pursue and develop his craft. Design should complement the work of the actor. At the moment very often the actor is overwhelmed by design. Theatres are built with design rather than actors in mind.

It is significant that the permanent staff at most theatres are technicians for lighting, sound, and set construction, stage management, wardrobe and administration whereas actors are employed on a casual basis, usually for one show at a time. The only security that the average actor has in terms of income is the guarantee that he is working for a rehearsal and performing period lasting usually for about eight weeks.

It is an incredibly perverse situation. The actor has little status and no security. It is my view that we get the actors and acting standards the profession supports.

What little design appears on the Noh stage – extra to the basic conventions of familiar costume and character – is made by the actors in training. In their early years as a Uchideshi, they learn how to construct the simple, but beautifully designed properties needed for each play. Just as they learn how to play the instruments, and work in the chorus, and act as attendants, so they learn the traditional elements of the design of their performance space and make direct contact with all its separate elements. They develop an awareness of its integrated whole, and their part in its design; there is no sense of alienation as there is, almost inevitably in the West.

Once the beautiful simplicity of the stage space is constructed, it remains basically the same for all performances of Noh. It is designed specifically for the Noh, and yet its architectural influence from the religious Shinto and Buddhist shrines and temples is immediately apparent. It has its taken-for-granted socio-historical and religious roots. The other supporting arts on display, are those of the mask carvers and the costume makers.

The rest, the drama, the creation of time and place and character and action, evolves magically before the audience, who are engaged in their imagination by the sublime skills of the performers. It is so obviously simple. We in the West choose to ignore the supreme example.

Mask presentation benefits from the same side-lighting, open-space designs which accompony dance in performance. It is these 'hoops' and corridors of side light which enhance the three-dimensional aspects of the masked performer.

I have included this brief digression on design, because I think it points to a fundamental problem that permeates all the other elements, which combine to make up much of the dulling experiences we usually have in

9. Performance space for mask with cross-lighting

our theatres. It leads me naturally onto the next brief detail – that of *Repertoire*.

Repertoire

Shakespeare remains the supreme western dramatist. However, in the extant folio versions which we use, the visual elements are left undisclosed. The when and where of exits and entrances offer little more in terms of the description of the action. This has encouraged academics to focus upon the complexity of language and meaning.

The staging therefore, of a Shakespeare text in our present-day theatres, is open to the same conjectural reconstruction which may accompany a modern Commedia. How some directors and actors have revealed Shakespeare's intent, in the design of their production is beyond me. It would seem that anything extravagant is worthy.

What we know of the Elizabethan playhouse leads us to believe that the staging was very basic (like the Noh) and the method of scene change equally symbolic and often emblematic. The focus was intimately upon the actor. Shakespeare wrote for a company of performers whose personality and skill he knew well, and whose financial and domestic life he probably managed: a sense of family.

What I feel instinctively is that the physicality of his texts is as yet largely unexplored. The genius of his playwriting is limited to an oral rendering. This whole cannon of incredibly dense theatre, provides the ultimate test for the western actor.

Actors in training must pound the beat with this material, day in and day out. There should be no day when some line or phrase of Shakespeare is not learned and explored and re-explored and re-learned. Why? Because it is simply the very best theatre writing that we have available in the English language. Shakespeare is our Zeami. New playwrights have to be persuaded to accommodate in their writing the skills of actors who are trained in the way I describe, who follow this additional physical philosophy and discipline.

We don't have to look any further than Samuel Beckett for a supreme, twentieth-century example of the playwright exploring the potential of physicality in his plays.

First the settings. Like his language, there is no indulgence in design extravagance. His sets are positively bleak in their emptiness. The focus upon the actor is total. Some crucial visual condition defines the actor's performing space. A leafless tree, a mound of confining earth, a tape recorder, a mouth; absolute in the precision of their theatrical purpose. His designs are exquisite.

I will dwell for a moment upon *Happy Days*. I think this play exemplifies, from existing material, a lot of what I have been proposing in terms of the physical dynamic which complements the rhythmical structure of the spoken language.

Winnie is buried in a pile of earth. Willie, her husband is almost visible behind it. She has with her a bag of properties; her world. He has his yellowing, page-turning newspaper. Each property is significant and useful by degree, whether it is actually handled like the toothbrush and paste, or whether it rests beside her untouched, like the gun, or is described in the imagination, like the passing Emmet.

On each page of script, the directions accompanying each movement and handling of the properties, is described with meticulous precision. It is not unusual to find three-quarters of a page of direction surrounding a quarter of dialogue. Patterns and rhythms and repetitions of language are matched by similar details of movement. Beckett knows – as a playwright should – how his words look, and ensures that his vision remains intact.

Playwrights like Beckett must become the mainstay of the classical repertoire, to which an actor should continually refer and sit with in front of the mirror – daily!

Removing the Mask, but Never Losing it

Much that I have written in this book makes a direct reference to the physical presence of the mask. In reality, this would eliminate in production ninety-nine percent of our dramatic literature in the West. What I have to say now is not a compromise to accommodate this state of affairs, but the final crucial statement upon which the thrust of my philosophy is based.

All characters, in all plays, should be prepared and presented with same sense of physical awareness and the same display of body skills as those prepared for the mask. This means that the repertoire of plays from Alan Ayckbourn to Harold Pinter, David Mamet to Edward Bond, Wole Soyinka to Michael Frayn are all available to the actor and the philosophy.

The mask provides the awareness and the way to the concept. With it physically removed, in his imagination and his intent, as a result of his training in the mask, the actor has to fill his conscious being with its presence and never deviate from its influence in the slightest detail.

Back to Infancy: The Beginnings

I referred earlier for the need to devise a method of training which matched in timescale and facility, that of music and dance. If a child in a small rural community, or industrial town wants to learn to play a brass instrument for instance, there is the instrument, the teaching, the ensemble playing, competition, examination, festival, Youth orchestra, professional tuition, sponsorship, and a clearly defined route to follow for those with a vocational potential and determination. Above all there is a graded library of music which matches exactly each stage of learning.

This facility is available as soon as it is required, but more naturally at the primary school age, through to entry into the profession as a full-time musician. It is a route which satisfies all the amateur and professional needs. Like the Noh, the professional is well supported by the amateur. Like the Noh, many professional musicians make themselves available, and pass on their learning and skills to the keen amateur.

Little of this is available for those interested in acting. And yet there are thousands of amateur acting groups in Britain all emulating (and in some cases surpassing in standard) their professional counterparts. But there are very few known, recognisable skills which they can learn. They instinctively mimic the acting clichés, and get much fun out of it. But never do they have a list of technical skills like musicians, which they can learn and test, and be acknowledged as possessing in performance. There is no sense of 'family' between the professional and the amateur actor.

There is an educational drama syllabus which occupies its place in the curriculum of many secondary schools. Some of the practical work includes the exploration of text via performance. Its status on the curriculum is increased if it is examinable, and fits into the General Certificate of Secondary Education, or the 'A' level Theatre Studies programme. If staff are trained to meet this programme then status, facility and time are granted accordingly.

In my view, the teaching of acting skills commensurate with those of music and dance does not exist.

In Primary schools, there is no curriculum drama. However, play-making and acting out, is considered a natural and vital part of play-ground and classroom learning. In the new documentation of instructions supplied to all primary schools by the Department of Education and Science, levels one and two of the *Speaking and Listening* module states that pupils 'should be able to participate as speakers and listeners in group activities, including imaginative play. Examples which are suggested include 'role play, story telling, enacting a poem, assume a role in play activity, and talk about characters'.

Here we find then, a Government statement which almost describes the early stages of learning about Drama and Theatre, although there is the familiar proviso that it is set within the framework of the English curriculum. There it rests as an *option*, with little more than the unskilled goodwill of enthusiastic teachers to enable its development.

If we look at music and dance we see that a specialist teacher of music has to have reached a high level of proficiency with their instrument even before they are accepted for teacher training; similarly with dance. Once trained, they work full time in schools or youth work or follow the peripatetic route, taking their skills to a group of schools on a fixed, timetabled schedule. Professional performers hold workshops and private lessons in addition to the state provision, to supplement their income. There is nothing resembling this for acting.

So this is where the philosophy of the mask has to begin. All the basic vocal, physical, mimetic and technical skills which I have described as being crucial to the philosophy, need to be prepared so as to relate to this first stage of natural play-making. Before this, we must train our professionals; our teachers, writers and directors.

A repertoire of dramatic material needs to be written which caters exclusively for the earliest beginnings and must accompany the programme of training until it reaches the existing repertoire. At this moment there is so little development and almost no encouragement in this direction, and there is in consequence an embarrassing absence of relevant, available material.

Work in schools has to relate to the work of Youth theatre, and also be linked, like sport, to the adult recreational activities of the amateur. What is experienced in the professional theatre is emulated by the enthusiastic amateur. Like the sense of family in Noh, the amateur and the professional must support and be inextricably linked with each other.

We must go back to our beginnings, re-determine the way, and make the art of professional acting a life-long process of dedicated learning and creativity. Give it worth and credibility bulging with skills and craft which no amateur could possibly emulate.

Put on the mask and begin again a way of life which is dominated by a passionate conviction of the power of the mask and the anonimity of the performer behind it which, activates the character of the mask with complete integrity and humility.

All masked characters are ghosts, spirits recreated in inanimate materials by the consummate skill of the actor wearing them. In this sense all characters in all plays are ghosts – especially those which are unmasked. If this is understood by actors, and they begin to submerge their egos in favour of their character they may discover how complex and demanding is their art and they may be convinced of the need to devote their lives to train and master it.

I have made generalised headings under which I would prepare such a programme of training. In the next three books I look more closely at specific influences upon my thinking and offer new resources and new plays which I think exemplify a positive way forward.

'Only the character of an actor formed by such a thorough training can know the seed of the Flower. For before he can know the Flower, he must know the seed. The Flower blooms from the imagination; the seed represents merely the various skills of our art'.[7]

In defining the way of the Flower, Zeami quotes lines from a Buddhist hymn, attributed to Hui-neng (638 – 713), the sixth Patriarch of Ch'an (Japanese Zen) Buddhism.

The mind-ground contains the various seeds, With the all-pervading rain each and every one sprouts. Once one has suddenly awakened to the sentiency of the flower, The fruit of enlightenment matures of itself.[8]

---

[7] Zeami, F. M. Foreword (11).   [8] Zeami, F. M. p. 30.

APPENDICES

(i) *The Mahabharata*

In the late winter and early spring of 1988 I was privileged as Artist in Residence to witness a metamorphosis which took place at the Old Transport Museum in Albert Street, Glasgow – that of the creation of a theatre designed specifically to house the travelling production of *The Mahabharata* directed by Peter Brook.

I arrived to begin my observations on the 29th February (Leap Year's Day) and I saw the performance on the 23rd April. Throughout I had a specific aim in view, to gain close access to Peter Brook, his team of actors and designers, and his philosophy.

I embarked upon a project which recorded in drawings and journal the creation of a theatre space of astonishing power and beauty; one which offered an open, infinitely versatile, uncluttered arena for the acting out of the epic narrative, and one which allowed for a real sense of intimacy for the audience.

The most extraordinary feature of the design was not the giant honeycomb of rough-rendered brick walls which shuttered and framed the acting area, but the baked earth floor which thrust itself into the belly of the auditorium.

I can recall watching the convoy of lorries dumping their cargoes into the raised brick perimeters; the mixing of the bales of straw to bind the clots of wet clay; the weeks of raking and rolling and drying; and marvelling at the finished result which, when lit in the straws and ambers of the Indian landscape, reflected the heat of the sun, and complemented so magically the colours of Indian silks.

What I discovered was that Brook takes his simple acting design with him wherever he travels. The Transport Museum in Glasgow became another version of the working home of Brook and his company in the Bouffes du Nord in Paris; a theatre stripped of its traditional ornate extravagance offering an uninterrupted, intimate focus upon the actor.

The small selection of drawings reproduced here reflect some of the incredible energy and skill which combined to complete this unforgettable project. What I absorbed from it has become as deeply influential as my ensuing experiences watching the Noh.

10a. The Tramway: main entrance

10b. Entrance hall. Iron pillars and girders

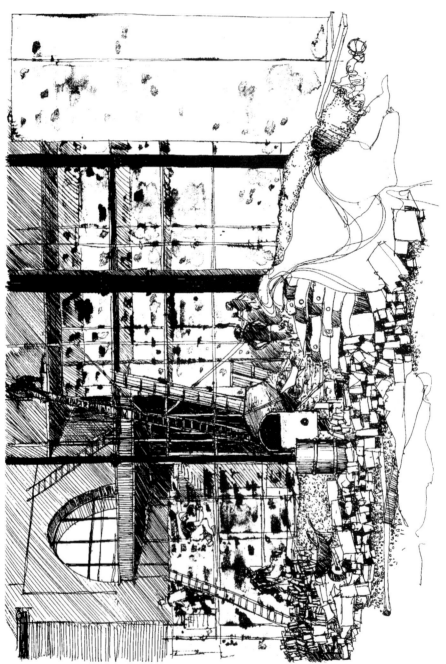

10c. The performance space. First impression

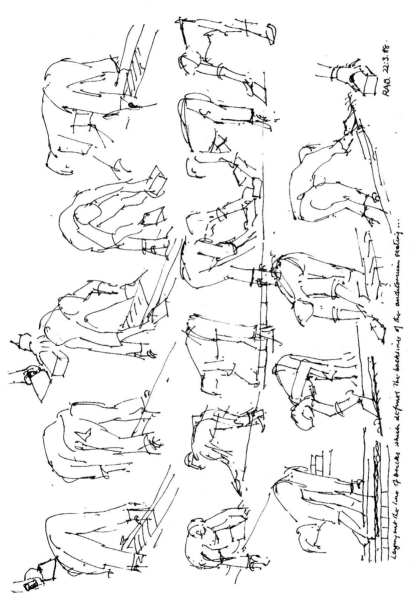

10d. Tens of thousands of bricks

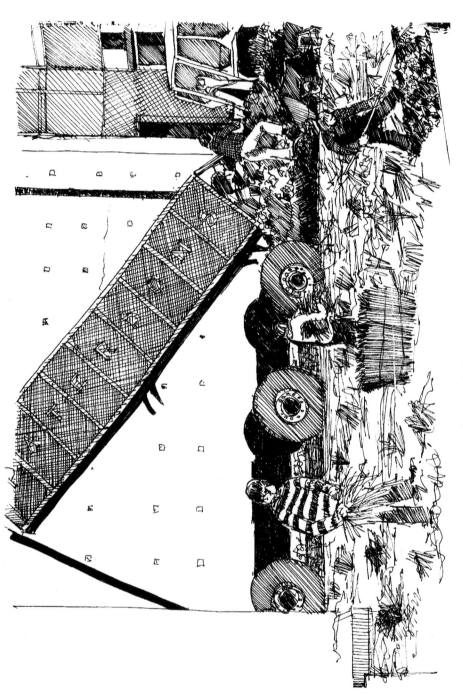

10e. Delivery of the clay and straw

10f. Raking out the acting area

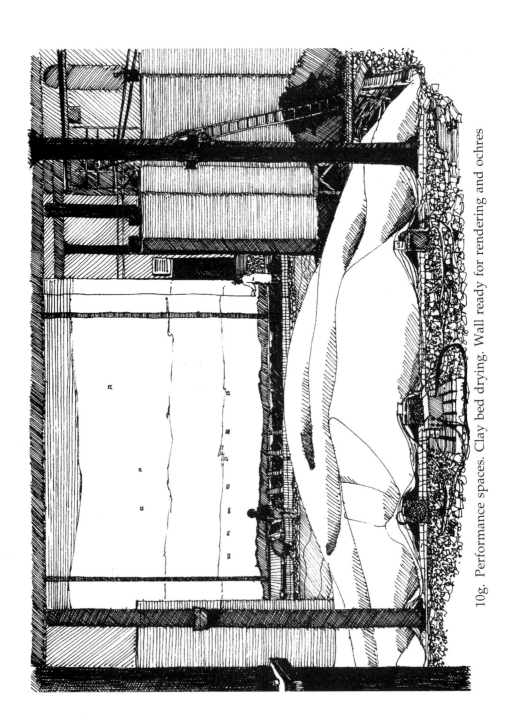

10g. Performance spaces. Clay bed drying. Wall ready for rendering and ochres

10h. Auditorium seating – first stage

10i. Revealing the clay bed – looking into the auditorium
– a theatre nearing completion

10j. The finished auditorium from the wings

(ii) Mask Making

There is extant evidence to support the fact that throughout the history of theatre, masks have been made from linen, leather, wood and clay. However, masks, like sculpture, can be made from most natural or man-made materials.

A 'mask' can in fact be created without covering the face with an inanimate shape. If the face is 'screwed up', distorted, and fixed (see ill. 11), it almost always pulls the rest of the body and the voice into line to accommodate its distortion. I have found this method very useful as way of introducing the concept of mask and its physicality, in performance – especially with young people.

11. Pulling faces

Two other ways of making a quick mask are a) by pressing a sheet of tin foil over a distorted face (see ill. 12) and b) by covering the head with a paper or carrier bag and tearing out the features (see ill. 13). In each case they are then removed so that the fixed expression can be assimilated and ways found to animate them physically (see 'Angles and attitudes', p. 40).

These 'instant' methods of making a crude and often effective mask enables the work on the body language which animates them to begin quickly.

However, there are many methods of making masks, all requiring different levels of artistic skill. The methods I describe will produce a durable performance-mask and its design and construction is within the capabilities of most people.

All of these masks are a version of the traditional papier mâché design. In my view this material is the most comfortable to wear as it is strong and light and allows the mask to 'breathe' when worn; it can become very hot under a mask in performance!

Although the masks are comparatively simple to make, they require time and patience. I am convinced that as a mask is turned over constantly during the various stages of its construction, a habit of reference will develop. This 'habit' becomes a crucial part of the rehearsal

12. Pressed tin foil

13. Paper bags

process whilst the distinctive elements of character are being established. Eventually the mask becomes the character and is the total reference.

(A) The Plaster Cast Method: Half-mask

A cast is made of the upper face from the above upper lip to the hair-line, leaving large holes for the eyes. The only technical information is that this casting will be made from plaster-impregnated bandage such as Gypsona bandage (available from chemists but needs to be ordered in advance) or the much cheaper Modrock.

Prepare the materials in advance (see ill. 14) and make sure that the area of the sitter is liberally protected with old newspapers or plastic sheeting. Plaster is notorious for 'travelling'! Arrange protective clothing barber-style for the sitters (see ill. 15). A shower cap is also useful.

Smear the upper face (especially the eyebrows and sideburns!) with a thin layer of Vaseline.

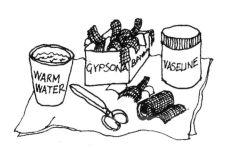

14. Materials and equipment needed for the Gypsona (or Modrock) method with gumstrip

Cut the bandage into small, manageable strips about 50mm 15mm. Dip these one at a time into a tumbler of warm water and apply two or three layers over the face leaving generous holes for the eyes. Cut the strips before hand so that continuous and speedy layering of the strips can take place.

It is also important when applying the strips to smooth them out immediately otherwise the outer surface can quickly become a landscape

15. Applying the strips of gypsona

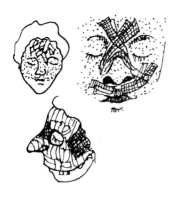

16. Extra layers across
nose and temples

17. Removing the cast

of warts which will make the next stage of covering the mask with paper more difficult.

Make sure also to add extra layers to the temples, and the criss-cross pattern across the bridge of the nose (see ill. 16) as these areas are especially vulnerable to fracture when the casting is removed.

By the time the last strip has been applied – after about twenty minutes – the cast is ready to be removed. Ease it away from the face by gently peeling it away from one side to the other (see ill. 17). At this stage, the casting is very fragile. *Its three-dimensional aspect must not be flattened*!

Allow it to dry (between 10 and 24 hours) and then seal each side with a coat of emulsion paint or PVC.

When the cast and sealer are dry, trim the rough edges with scissors and cover *both sides* of the casting with a couple of layers of gumstrip strips. When dry, this forms the basic form upon which the specific design of the character is built. It is this part of the process which in my view instantly overcomes the problems of creating the three-dimensional aspect of the mask. By taking a casting of a face this has already been achieved.

The details of the personality of the mask are then considered, and it is at this point that the basic codes of expression are drawn out before the features are attached. I am always drawn to the skill of the cartoonist who finds in each character a dominant feature which seems to pull the rest of the face into line with it (see ill. 18). Once the line of the eye or twist of the mouth has been determined the other lines of jaw cheek and forehead complement and add power to the original.

18. Cartoons of expression

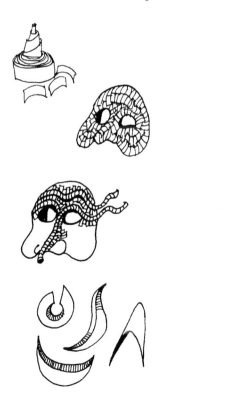

19. Attaching the features with masking tape – covering with gumstrip

It is the drawing out of the features which form the personality of the character that poses the most difficult problems for the designer, and the essential elements are constantly under review and changing as the rehearsal process develops.

However, once some of the provisional design features like noses and eyes have been established, the details of their structure are attached with masking tape, using rope, string, paper sculpture (see ill. 19), and eventually covered with more gumstrip.

Trim the edges of the mask so that they follow the direction and angles of the eyebrows, to reinforce by their simple repetition, the clarity of the overall design.

Keep looking at the profile to make sure that the lines (at the nostrils for instance) also flow into the lines at the lower cheeks and run smoothly up the jawline to the ears.

Small pieces of sponge or soft material can be stuck to parts of the inside of the mask (usually the bridge of the nose or cheek) to lift it off the face slightly to make it fit more comfortably. Ties of black tape about 25mm wide are secured firmly at the temple area and checked for stability when tied (see ill. 20).

If the mask is to be 'framed' in performance by hats, beards, moustaches, cloaks or wigs, or even by hands (see ill. 21) then these elements should be continually referred to and tested against the mask as it is being assembled.

When painting the mask, do not over-elaborate with an assortment of lines and colours. The mask should work under lights as a piece of

sculpture, creating its own lines and shadows as it moves.

I tend to paint them simply in subtle shades of one colour; lighter on the 'hills' and darker in 'valleys'. Don't be tempted to draw lines on raised wrinkles or eyebrows for instance, this can reverse the effect of the modelling. I usually paint with a matt emulsion as gloss reflects the light.

20. The finished half-mask

21. Framing the mask ...

(B) Sculptured Card

This method is no more difficult than method (A) and much of the building up of the features is done in the same way. The first stage is to

72

make a simple 'visor' upon which to attach the features. The same need to prepare a comfortable three-dimensional base prevails. This method tends to encourage a bolder, more stylised design than (A) because of the way the cruder base mask is constructed.

(i) It is simple to create a cone which fits snugly over the performer's head from a flat piece of thin card. In the diagram opposite you will notice that the cone has been pulled into a shape which also has a kind of visor at the front (see ill. 22).

22. Card sculpture with cones

You will find this shape easy to create and easier to identify the front of the mask upon which the features are attached. Secure the edges either with staples (covered with gumstrip) or masking-tape.

Once the features have been attached then the residue can be cut away as in (A) or used as a framework to support a switch of hair or wig.

(ii) Cut a card strip 6cm wide which is long enough to fit around the head. Staple the ends together to form a 'halo' and cover the staples with gumstrip.

Cut a rectangle of card (visor) which covers the face from below the lower lip to the ears, and staple to the 'halo' (see ill. 23).

Mark and cut out small holes for the eyes, and also a slit at the front which when bent back will form flaps to attach a nose shape and also allow the wearer's nose through the rectangle of card.

Make a nose shape from a triangle of card which is larger than you think you need; the wider the triangle base the further it will protrude from the face. Use masking tape to attach the nose.

Adopting similar techniques described in (A) form the features, trim the excess and add the ties (see ill. 24).

Another simple mask base can be made by wrapping long strips of

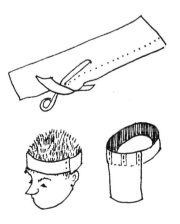

23. 'Halo' and visor

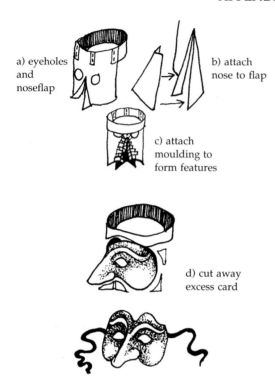

a) eyeholes
and
noseflap

b) attach
nose to flap

c) attach
moulding to
form features

d) cut away
excess card

24. From visor to completion

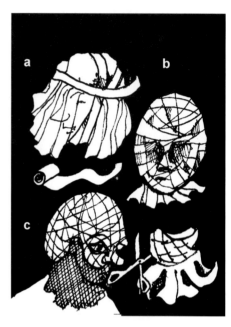

25. Gumstrip and tissue mummies:
a) gumstrip bands; b) tissue; c) cut
away excess to produce half-mask

gumstrip around a tissue-covered head, again leaving holes for the eyes, nose and mouth (see ill. 25). This is a particularly useful way of creating an instant three-dimensional base for a full mask upon which switches or twigs are attached. Once again this 'mummy' is cut and trimmed to fit over the head, features added, and can be pulled securely over the wearer with the 'skull-cap' element left intact, or trimmed to the familiar mask designs shown of (A) and (B) with ties attached.

A mask can also be made by cutting the features out of a triangular piece of hessian, and pulling it around the face, trying it like a bandana. In this case (see ill. 26) twigs and pine leaves have been attached to a tightly fitting hat to frame the mask.

Masks can cover the face and be tied to it or supported on the roof of the head and secured beneath the chin with ties (see ill. 27). They can of course be engineered to sit on the shoulders of the wearers and strapped on like a rucksack if the scale and height of the masks are of giant proportions.

The more traditional methods of mask design and making require a high degree of skill and experience in working such materials as wood

26a. Cloth mask

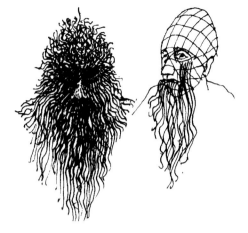

26b. Mummified full mask

27. Through and under the mask.
Plaster-cast and card method

and leather. In Volume 2 the carving of a Noh mask is diagrammatically explained, and in Volume 3 the processes involved in making a leather Commedia mask are similarly described.

All I have tried to do in this appendix is to offer encouragement to those wishing to explore and experiment with mask using the philosophy and methods described, with little or no artistic experience, in the hope that they will not shy at the first mask-making hurdle. In fact masks don't have to be made. With the minimum of imaginative enterprise, they can be created by adapting the most unlikely articles of clothing or objects.

INDEX

INDEX

Shinto, 50
Soyinka, Wole, 53
Speech, 3, 6, 22, 32, 44, 45
Stanislvski, Konstantin
   Sergeivich, 3, 5–9, 26

Tag Teatro, 29
Tara Arts, 3

Teachers, 1, 2, 3, 29, 30, 31, 32, 54,
   see also Stanislavski, 5 and
   Meyerhold, 13
Théâtre de Complicité, 29
Trestle Theatre Company, 3, 39

Zeami, Motokiyu, 49, 52, 55